"This book is invaluable for American citizens wanting practical advice for how they can help bring people together to save our precious democracy."

—**Dick Gephardt,** *Former Democratic Leader, U.S. House of Representatives*

"Every so often in our history, America reinvents herself, usually to make room. In *Remaking the Space Between Us*, Smith lays out the responsibility we have as citizens and patriots to create opportunities for all, not just some. Drawing on historical and social science research, Smith explains how we got to where we are and how citizens across the country, often unnoticed, are working together to find a way forward for all of us. Looking for ways to build a better America? Read this book!"

—**Deval L. Patrick,** *Professor of Practice and Co-Director of the Center for Public Leadership at the Harvard Kennedy School of Government, Former Governor of Massachusetts*

"In *Remaking the Space Between Us*, Diana McLain Smith brings an extraordinary range of sources and insights to bear on the foremost challenge that America now confronts. Drawing on her deep and varied experience, she not only sheds light on what has gone wrong in our common life—she also offers concrete steps we each can take to make things better. This is an essential guidebook for our time."

—**Yuval Levin,** *American Enterprise Institute*

"Starved for hope? Find it here. Practical and pointed, this book plumbs the social sciences to understand the spaces between us, then plumbs our world to find people remaking those spaces to bring us together."

—**Jane Mansbridge,** *Adams Professor of Political Leadership and Democratic Values, Emerita, Harvard Kennedy School of Government*

"Amid our national crisis, most of our attention is focused on the failures of our leaders, the authoritarians threatening to take away our freedoms, and the institutions ideally designed to save us. Not enough attention is being placed on our complicity in this crisis as citizens. Dr. Diana Smith makes a critical contribution to closing that gap in *Remaking the Space Between Us*, writing: 'Today one of the biggest risks to our democracy lies not just in our leaders but in our own corrosive behavior as citizens.' This is a hard truth that needs to be said in a timely and important book that needs to be read. In it lies lessons for all of us on how we as citizens have both agency and responsibility to close the spaces between us to ensure that our government of the people, by the people, and for the people endures."

—**Ian Bassin,** *Executive Director, Protect Democracy*

"One thing people on the left, right, and center all agree on is that American democracy is in peril. If you're in one of those categories, this may be the most important book you'll read this year."

—**Sheila Heen,** *Professor of Negotiation at Harvard Law School, Co-Author of* New York Times *bestsellers* Difficult Conversations *and* Thanks for the Feedback

"*Remaking the Space Between Us* is refreshing, honest, and challenging. The inclusion of history and the impact of race distinguishes this work from anything similar."

—**James Gee,** *Founder, Stono Public Affairs*

"*Remaking the Space Between Us* offers a valuable prescription for hopelessness and division, speaking to two fundamental truths. First, we are not simply observers in the dysfunction and division we see. Rather, we have agency. As President Kennedy put it, 'In a democracy, every citizen, regardless of his interest in politics, "holds office"; every one of us is in a position of responsibility.' And second, our path forward requires recognizing that we are all in the same boat—that we are more likely to get where we want to go if, rather than using our oars to beat each other over the heads, we listen and learn and figure out how to row together in the same direction."

—**Congressman Derek Kilmer**

"In Diana Smith's timely book on how to depolarize America, she has given us a recipe for hope through common sense. *Remaking the Space Between Us* is a practical guide for people who want to prepare for peace, inspiring us to break out of our echo chambers. Readers will feel charged to answer the dual question that lies at the center of the book: who are we, and who do we want to be?"

—**Samar Ali,** *Research Professor of Law and Political Science at Vanderbilt University, Founding CEO of Millions of Conversations, Co-Chair on Vanderbilt University's Project on Unity and American Democracy*

"This provocative group of essays prods us to take responsibility for the dismal state of our politics and act not by getting angry but by getting interested. It calls on Americans to stop caricaturing and get curious in order to close the space between us. A hopeful book that restores our agency, these are words America needs now."

—**Dr. Rachel Kleinfeld,** *Senior Fellow in the Democracy, Conflict, and Governance Program, Carnegie Endowment for International Peace*

"Politics, at its core, is about groups. *Remaking the Space Between Us* plunges readers into the depths of group dynamics in democracies. Smith crafts a meticulously researched narrative on the anatomy of societal divisions, challenging readers to rethink the boundaries that separate us and to embrace the power of cooperative evolution. For those searching for ways to repair our fractured political landscape, this book is an essential compass."

—**Lee Drutman,** *Senior Fellow, New America, Political Reform Program*

"If you've ever wondered how we can heal our fractured society, *Remaking the Space Between Us* strikes an encouraging note. Smith's book is a timely call to action, reminding us that, despite our differences, we share more than we lack: a common humanity that will be our saving grace."

—**Alan Coffee,** *Commentator and Researcher, King's College London*

"In *Remaking the Space Between Us*, Diana Smith provides useful guidance for how we, as citizens, can exercise our agency to be a force for positive change by embracing the enormous responsibility and power of citizenship. Smith invites us to challenge our beliefs about a zero-sum world so we can build a more inclusive and pluralistic democracy. This is a must-read for 21st century Americans!"

—**Yordanos Eyoel,** *Founder and CEO, Keseb*

"Smith isn't urging us to figure out how to fix the mess we're in; she demonstrates with a compelling mix of stories and statistics that we already know what to do. We, the people, just have to step up and do it. A good place to start? Read this book with a neighbor—whether friend or foe—and talk it through. Agree, disagree, grapple, argue, learn, all while keeping an eye on the fact that as Americans, and as human beings, we're all in this together."

—**Douglas Stone,** *Co-Author of* New York Times *bestsellers* Difficult Conversations *and* Thanks for the Feedback

"The stories and people in *Remaking the Space Between Us* give us a way out of the escalating conflict, trauma, and hate that harms us all. If ever we needed this book, it is now."

—**Patrice O'Neill,** *Founder and CEO of Not in Our Town, Filmmaker*

"This book lays bare the uncomfortable truth that we will never be able to resolve divisions across groups until we look within our own groups and reflect on how we're contributing to the breakdown. This was a key insight in my learning as an executive while leading a large, diverse organization."

—**Susan Asiyanbi,** *Founder and CEO of The Olori Network, Former Chief Operating and Program Officer at Teach for America*

REMAKING *the* SPACE BETWEEN US

HOW CITIZENS
CAN WORK
TOGETHER TO
BUILD A
BETTER FUTURE
FOR ALL

DIANA McLAIN SMITH

Ballast Books, LLC
www.ballastbooks.com

ISBN: 978-1-962202-31-2

Printed in the United States of America

Cover Design by Claire Sullivan
Cover Art by Vadym Malyshevskyi
Layout by Suzanne Uchytil

Published by Ballast Books
www.ballastbooks.com

For more information, bulk orders, appearances, or speaking requests, please email:
info@ballastbooks.com

In memory of Omari Todd—

"Mission Accomplished"

For all those who attend to
the humanity of humans.

Our hope lies with you.

The real question is whether the brighter future is really always so distant. What if, on the contrary, it has been here for a long time already, and only our own blindness and weakness has prevented us from seeing it around us and within us, and kept us from developing it?

—Václav Havel, "The Power of the Powerless"

Not everything that is faced can be changed, but nothing can be changed until it is faced.

—James Baldwin, "As Much Truth As One Can Bear"

CONTENTS

The POWER of the POWERLESS[1]

These essays are for people who long for a better future but cannot see their way through the obstacle course our democracy has become. We are among the 87 percent wedged between the 13 percent on the far right and left. We hold a wide range of views across the political spectrum that are more flexible and pragmatic than the ideologically committed.[2] Many of us worry it might be too late. Some are growing indifferent or cynical. Many others feel powerless.

It is easy to see why. The past fifty years have unleashed one disruptive change after another, from globalization to mass migration to global warming to worsening inequalities and tribalism, all of it culminating in contested elections, tumultuous presidencies, and a pandemic. Small wonder so many of us have grown hypersensitive to threat and prone to pessimism.[3]

At the same time, news of our nation's polarization is so omnipresent that it can hardly be called news. The refrain is so common that many of us assume it is simply an inevitable part of American life, to be regretted or ignored but not changed, at least not by us. Since that assumption runs the risk of creating a

---

[1] Václav Havel's catalytic essay "The Power of the Powerless" has inspired many, including me.

[2] More in Common, "Hidden Tribes of America: A Study of America's Polarized Landscape," 2018. https://hiddentribes.us.

[3] David Brooks, "Why Biden Isn't Getting the Credit He Deserves," *New York Times,* June 21, 2023.

self-fulfilling prophecy—"if there is nothing I can do, I need not do anything"—
it begs two questions:

- How polarized are we, really?
- How open to learning and change are we, really?

**Our answers to these two questions matter. Only by coming
together and learning from each other can we make something
good out of the disruptive changes transforming our world.**

My research suggests that the most useful answers to these questions come
from citizens countering the misperceptions, insular thinking, and social distance
that feed polarization and starve learning. What they are discovering will both
surprise and inspire you.

How polarized are we, really?

In 2018, a citizen-led nonprofit called More in Common launched the Hidden
Tribes of America project to better understand polarization in the United States
and to galvanize citizens to counteract it. Their research is helping us see just
how wrong our answers to this first question are. In their inaugural 2018 report,
they refuted the widespread belief that our different views are concentrated on
opposing extremes. Turns out, only 13 percent of the population hold views on
the extreme ends. The rest of us—a whopping 87 percent—hold views along a
more flexible and pragmatic continuum.[4]

In another study, they uncovered a significant perception gap between what
Republicans and Democrats think members of the other party believe and what
they actually believe.[5] They found that both parties overestimate the percentage of
people in the other party who hold what they consider extreme views—*and by twice
as much.* On attitudes toward democracy, they discovered that roughly eight in ten
Americans, both before and after the 2020 election, still prefer democracy over
other types of governments. Most Americans view democracy as a fundamental
part of their identity, support democracy over alternatives, remain engaged in the
system, respect democracy's foundations, and believe in and long for greater unity.[6]

---

[4] More in Common, "Hidden Tribes."

[5] More in Common, "The Perception Gap." 2019. https://perceptiongap.us.

[6] More in Common, "Attitudes Toward Democracy," 2021. https://www.moreincommon.com/attitudes
-toward-democracy/.

More recently, a 2023 poll conducted by the Vanderbilt Project on Unity and American Democracy found similar results. They show a surprising amount of consensus on a range of controversial issues, from gun control to climate change to raising the debt ceiling to the use of the abortion pill mifepristone.[7] A year earlier, a research article summarized seven studies that reveal how people consistently underestimate the willingness of disagreeing counterparts to learn from opposing views.[8]

All of this suggests that we are not as polarized, extreme, or closed as many of us think. So why do so many of us think we are? The folks at More in Common believe it is because:

> **Vocal partisan voices are drowning out the more complex, less strident views held by a more flexible and pragmatic majority open to listening, learning, and changing their minds.[9]**

If that is right, it suggests we need to find ways to stop the most vocal partisan voices from dominating our national conversation. We need to find out what different members of this more flexible, pragmatic majority think—*and* how open they are to learning and to changing their minds after talking through the issues with one another.

How open to learning and change are we, really?

Two researchers at Stanford's Deliberative Democracy Lab, James Fishkin and Larry Diamond, decided to find out by conducting experiments in what they call "deliberative democracy." In these experiments, citizens are briefed on issues voters deem important, then talk directly with one another about how best to address them. Two experiments conducted in 2019 and 2021 were remarkably ingenious. Both aimed to find out what happens when well-informed citizens discuss contentious issues with one another without strident partisan voices dominating the conversation. Unlike experiments that show how quickly and intractably we polarize, these experiments were designed to see if citizens would polarize less under different circumstances. Specifically, the researchers wanted to know how a representative

---

[7] Vanderbilt Project on Unity and American Democracy's Unity Poll Results, 2023. https://t.e2ma.net /message/7yywek/7q8i033.

[8] Hanne K. Collins, Charles A. Dorison, Francesca Gino, and Julia A. Minson, "Underestimating Counterparts' Learning Goals Impairs Conflictual Conversations," Psychological Science, 2022, 1–21.

[9] More in Common, "Attitudes Toward Democracy."

sample of citizens think, feel, and act when participating in an evidence-based dialogue across party, ideology, and identity.[10]

Their first experiment brought together in one room the most statistically diverse group in American history, after randomly selecting a representative sample of 523 registered voters from around the country. For four days in Dallas, Texas, this group of citizens deliberated on five issues singled out by voters as the most important: immigration, healthcare, the economy, the environment, and foreign policy. The results were stunning. On all five issues, the most polarizing proposals lost support while the more moderate proposals gained support, in some cases overwhelming support: 80 percent of participants supported expanding the earned income tax credit to more middle-class workers, and 70 percent favored using taxes or other market incentives to achieve emissions reductions. Most striking, proposals on the right generally lost support from Republicans, while proposals on the left generally lost support from Democrats.

Two years later during the pandemic, the Lab brought together 926 randomly selected citizens to deliberate for two days in a virtual room on a single issue: climate policy. The organizers gave participants a sixty-four-page briefing with the pros and cons of different proposals for reaching net-zero greenhouse gases by 2050, then broke them down into small groups of 10 to 12 to deliberate. Polling at the beginning and end of the two days again showed both Democrats and Republicans shifting, with conservatives moving from minority to majority consensus on eliminating greenhouse gases from coal, ideally by 2035, and Democrats moving slightly to favor nuclear power plants being part of the "future energy mix."

Some of the most telling results, however, came from two participants whose reflections after the first experiment captured the sentiments of others:

> "My opinions have changed more toward the center than toward any one side," noted a tattooed man in a cowboy hat from Colorado. "The country is not as divided as the media make it seem."

> "This has been an incredible journey, to sit in a room and have a conversation and not have to worry," one woman reflected in her final small-group discussion. "I'd like to see our politicians sit down with the same rules: You're not disrespectful or unkind to anyone."[11]

---

[10] This account is based on James Fishkin and Larry Diamond, "This Experiment Has Some Great News for Our Democracy," *New York Times,* October 2, 2019, and Talib Visram, "What happens when you put 926 random Americans in a room and tell them to solve the climate crisis," *Fast Company,* October 26, 2021.
[11] Ibid.

You're not disrespectful or unkind to anyone. Just imagine it. Keep in mind, these results came in the midst of a presidency and a pandemic that was turning almost all of us into wingnuts. Still, they did precede an even more polarizing time after January 6, when we failed to transfer power peacefully from one president to another, and when 70 percent of Republican voters thought the election was rigged due to widespread voter fraud.[12] Since then, some Republican legislators in Congress and over half of our states have sought legislation that would restrict the vote, once again turning voting rights into a battleground for democracy.

That is likely why Fishkin and Diamond focused their most recent experiment on voting. They wanted to test the widely accepted view that partisan differences around voting had become so entrenched that they were immovable.[13] Although the pandemic no longer prevented them from bringing Americans together in one room, they decided to see if virtual deliberations, supported by technology, would allow them to scale their efforts. Turns out, they do.

In June 2023, Fishkin and Diamond assembled a representative sample of 600 citizens in a virtual room to deliberate on voting. This time, they used an AI-assisted platform in their 10-person groups to ensure civility and equal participation and to help identify questions for a panel of competing experts. They found the same results. On every topic, from online voter registration to people's perceptions of voter fraud to ensuring accurate vote counts to electoral reforms like ranked-choice voting, members of both parties modified their views, moving closer to one another and toward solutions both parties might accept: "When Americans take the time to talk to each other in a civil, evidence-based way," say Fishkin and Diamond, "they learn to listen to each other and often change their views dramatically, depolarizing across partisan divides."

The point here is not that participants moved toward the center, though many did. The point is that Americans are not as entrenched as we are led to believe. Most of us are still open to learning and to changing our views when not intoxicated by those loud, highly partisan voices blasted 24/7 over cable TV and social media. Once free of that madding crowd, we are quite capable of making well-informed, deliberately considered judgments. Two citizens, Fishkin and Diamond, cared enough to find that out and tell the rest of us.

---

[12] "Voters' Reflections on the 2020 Election," Pew Research Center, https://rb.gy/fm3qv.

[13] This account is based on James Fishkin and Larry Diamond, "Can deliberation cure our divisions about democracy?" *Boston Globe,* August 21, 2023.

What can you and I do?

No doubt our nation and our democracy are in a precarious position, as are we, its stewards and beneficiaries. We are growing dangerously closer within groups and more distant across groups, causing a rise in polarization since 2000 that is threatening our democracy's future.[14] Still, when perched on a sheer rock face without a rope, it does not help to rivet our attention on how steep the climb is, on how likely it is that we will fall, or on who is to blame if we do. And yet most news accounts and opinion pieces today do exactly that by:

- Focusing on factors outside our control.

- Making predictions about how likely it is our democracy or humanity will meet its end.

- Casting blame for our impending demise on one or another party, politician, or policy.

Far from preparing us, these accounts are sowing so much despair and fear that most of us are too exhausted or enraged to do anything, at least anything constructive. These essays counter this tendency by defining a problem you and I can solve.

> **They show why we need not—and why we must not—give up on each other or give in to forces so overwhelming they make us feel powerless. We are not powerless.**

Of all the players vying to shape our fate—elected officials, social media, twenty-four-hour cable news, extremists on the left and right—citizens from different groups, working together toward a common goal, have the greatest incentive and wherewithal to get us out of this mess.

Citizens who understand this are already coming together in communities across our nation to bring a vision of America into existence that acknowledges and embraces the multigroup nature of our democracy. Though you would never know it from reading or listening to the news, they number in the *tens of thousands,* making up a locally rooted and nationally connected social movement of "unlikely allies" across race, place, gender, class, age, sector, and party. Among those within this movement are grassroots community groups,

---

[14] Byungkyu Lee and Peter Bearman, "Political isolation in America," *Network Science*, vol. 8, no. 3 (2020): 333–355.

academics and researchers, members of law enforcement, social media experts, filmmakers, journalists, Christians, Muslims, Jews, Hindus, straight people and gay people, business people, union members, even those working within the halls of Congress.[15]

History has demonstrated time and again the power of citizens to change the course of events for the better. It was citizens working together toward a common goal who:

- Turned the tide of World War II by sailing a fleet of small boats across the English Channel to rescue 300,000 soldiers stranded on the shores of Dunkirk.

- Pioneered a nonviolent mass resistance movement that freed India from British rule.

- Built an abolitionist movement that ended slavery in the U.S. and extended the rights and protections of citizenship to Black men.

- Organized a nonviolent, decades-long civil rights movement that outlawed segregation and got voting rights passed a century later.

- Lobbied, lectured, wrote, and protested as part of a suffrage movement that amended the U.S. Constitution to extend the right to vote to women.

- Launched a labor movement in Poland that precipitated the collapse of the Soviet Union.

- Brought down a military dictatorship and restored democracy to Argentina.

- Ended legal apartheid in South Africa after decades of struggle.

- Fought to establish a democracy in America through a war of independence, to save it through a civil war, and to defend it through two world wars.

- Mobilized in a day to resist Russia's invasion of Ukraine, inspiring a worldwide fight for democracy.

The list goes on, each time taking us by surprise, because few expect so much from those we think of as having so little.

---

[15] Cf. Movement Building in Rachel Kleinfeld's "Five Strategies to Support U.S. Democracy."

Perhaps that is why, in times like ours when so many of us feel helpless, we forget that it was the combined power of citizens that led each of these nations out of darkness.

> **We forget that our power as citizens lies not just in our rights as individuals but in our responsibilities as a people for working together to build a better future.**

It is our turn to take up the work left undone by these past movements. "I still believe that we can do with this country something that has not been done before," said a weary but undeterred James Baldwin at another low point in our history as a nation. "We are misled here because we think of numbers. You don't need numbers; you need passion."[16]

If we ignite that passion in one another and wed it to an understanding of where we've been, where we need to go, and how to get there, nothing can stop us.

---

[16] From the documentary *I Am Not Your Negro* based on James Baldwin's writings and interviews.

PART 1

REMEMBERING

the

FORGOTTEN ROAD

to

NOW

History, as nearly no one seems to know, is not merely something to be read. And it does not refer merely, or even principally, to the past. On the contrary, the great force of history comes from the fact that we carry it within us, are unconsciously controlled by it in many ways, and history is literally present in all that we do.

—James Baldwin

Busy remaking the world, man forgot to remake himself.

—Andrei Platonov

ONE

OUR EVOLUTIONARY LEGACY

Never in recent times have our tribal tendencies as a species been more on display than during the COVID-19 pandemic. "What catastrophes seem to do—sometimes in the span of a few minutes—is turn back the clock on 10,000 years of social evolution," writes Sebastian Junger in *Tribe*. "Self-interest gets subsumed into group interest because there is no survival outside group survival."[17] Research conducted by evolutionary anthropologist Michael Tomasello and his colleagues reveals how humans moved early on from rudimentary individual collaboration to more sophisticated group-level cooperation to successfully compete against other groups.[18] This means something that often gets overlooked: these two human potentialities—cooperation and competition—emerged hand in hand, the one reinforcing the other.

Much has been written about how we have evolved as a species to both cooperate and compete, to both empathize and fear.[19] Clearly the potential for both lies within us. But at least *at this stage in our evolution, cooperation and empathy are much more likely to flourish within groups while competition, even hate, is much more likely to break out across groups.*[20]

---

[17] Sebastian Junger, *Tribe: On Homecoming and Belonging* (New York: Twelve, 2016), Kindle Ed., 65.

[18] Michael Tomasello, Alicia P. Melis, Claudio Tennie, Emily Wyman, and Ester Herrmann, "Two Key Steps in the Evolution of Human Cooperation: The Interdependence Hypothesis," *Current Anthropology*, vol. 53, no. 6 (December 2012).

[19] See Robert M. Smith, *Primal Fear: Tribalism, Empathy, and the Way Forward* (Santa Barbara: Windance Press LLC, 2021).

[20] I use the term "group" in these essays to refer to people who are located close together and/or who others class together (see *Oxford Languages*). Though we all belong to multiple groups, the strength of our ties to these groups vary, as does their influence over us, determining the group or groups with whom we most strongly self-identify.

Why is this? Why has this early evolutionary legacy survived all the way up to today? I believe the most useful answer lies in how you and I define the space between us through our everyday interactions within and across groups. As research on polarization shows, the closer we grow within groups—interacting regularly, believing the same things, tethering our identities to the group—*and* the more distant groups become from one another—rarely interacting, believing different things, building different identities—the more likely it is that cooperation and empathy will flourish within groups and competition and animosity will break out across groups. [21]

In many democracies today, including ours, these opposing tendencies are escalating ever faster, creating greater solidarity within groups and greater polarization across groups. In research on social networks in the U.S., sociologists Byungkyu Lee and Peter Bearman detected a sharp rise in political isolation across groups and political like-mindedness within groups in 2016, a trend that has not abated since then. "We're segregating physically away from one another into our tribes and virtually in terms of the media that we consume," says conflict expert Peter T. Coleman. "That's a major concern because we've learned from research for decades that . . . when you have regular everyday contact with people who are different from you, it mitigates the escalation of intergroup conflict." [22] Byungkyu and Bearman's research shows a similar result: people with larger, more diverse networks have more accurate political knowledge, are more likely to vote, and have greater exposure to ideological diversity. [23]

Our current trend toward greater cross-group distance is renewably powered by collusion cliques, or in today's parlance, "echo chambers," those closed, insular groups that recycle views and rarely dispute them. The rise of digital media since 2000 has turbocharged animosity among these cliques, not by reinforcing their views but by exposing them to conflicting views online without the moderating effects of face-to-face interaction. Turns out, the more cliques are exposed to competing views online, absent face-to-face contact, the more they will cling to

[21] For some of the best research on polarization, see Peter T. Coleman's *The Way Out: How to Overcome Toxic Polarization* (New York: Columbia University Press, 2021); Ezra Klein's *Why We're Polarized* (New York: Simon and Schuster, 2020); and Maiese, Michelle, Tova Norlen, and Heidi Burgess, "Polarization," *Beyond Intractability*. Eds. Guy Burgess and Heidi Burgess, Conflict Information Consortium, University of Colorado, Boulder. Posted: October 2003.

[22] Heather Graci, Interview with Peter T. Coleman, *Behavioral Scientist,* June 2021, https://behavioralscientist.org/toxic-polarization-feeds-on-simplicity-peter-coleman-offers-complexity-as-a-way-out/.

[23] Lee Byungkyu and Peter Bearman, 2020. They cite Lake & Huckfeldt, 1998, Mutz, 2002, and Huckfeldt et al., 2004.

their views.[24] That, as we see today, is a recipe not only for distorting the truth, but for never *learning* that we are distorting the truth. That is a big problem, warned political theorist Hannah Arendt: "The ideal subject of totalitarian rule is not the convinced Nazi or the dedicated communist, but people for whom the distinction between fact and fiction . . . no longer exists."[25]

Closing the distance across groups, then, requires us to open up the space within groups, so individual identities can flourish, as can ideas or facts that go against the group's orthodoxy, making groups less monolithic. That is no easy task, as Peter Coleman knows. "Humans form group preferences quickly, and groups tend toward conformity and extremity. We all tend to favor our in-groups . . . and to disfavor and discriminate against out-groups. Even when groups are based on nothing more than coin tosses or estimates of the number of jelly beans in a jar, we quickly show in-group favoritism."[26] And, as we all know from history, once a group bands together in opposition to groups they hate or fear, our ability to think plummets, leading us to cling ever tighter to those like us and to reject, oppress, even kill those not like us.

How do you and I figure in all of this?

Many of us already know or at least intuit much of this. Yet it is difficult for us to see our own role in creating this reality, just as it was for members of an organization where I once led a change effort. In interviews, everyone agreed that the organization was producing more conflict and turmoil than strategic clarity or impact. But a subsequent survey surfaced a puzzling asymmetry: while most people were aware of what others were doing to create results no one liked, they were largely unaware of what they themselves were doing. The asymmetry was staggering. Seventy-eight percent said they delivered on commitments while only 35 percent of everyone else did; 58 percent said they addressed performance problems directly while only 14 percent of everyone else did; 59 percent said that they learned from disagreements while only 8 percent of everyone else did—and on it went, as Table 1.1 shows.

---

[24] Cf. Petter Törnberg, "How digital media drive affective polarization through partisan sorting," PNAS, 119(42) October 18, 2022, https://rb.gy/v71ef.

[25] Hannah Arendt, *The Origins of Totalitarianism* (New York: Mariner Books, New Edition, 1976), Kindle Ed., 475.

[26] Coleman, *The Way Out*, 56.

Table 1.1: Other Survey Results

	Most think they are better than others at:	Myself	Others
Learning	Raising concerns directly.	49%	10%
	Discussing mistakes openly.	63%	25%
	Learning from disagreements.	59%	8%
	Handling ambiguity.	80%	17%
	Learning from people who cause them frustration.	29%	2%
	Most think they are better than others at:	**Myself**	**Others**
Performance	Delivering on commitments.	78%	35%
	Addressing performance problems.	58%	14%
	Meeting deadlines.	69%	25%
	Knowing what they are accountable for.	82%	14%

The statistical impossibility was obvious to everyone: a large percentage of people cannot be doing something they say happens only a small percentage of the time. The implication was equally obvious: people were far more aware of what their colleagues were doing than what they themselves were doing to contribute to the problems they saw. For the first time, groups up, down, and across the hierarchy realized that they were together creating a reality none of them wanted. And for the first time, they saw that changing that reality would require all of them to change, together.

I bet if we conducted a similar survey of U.S. citizens, we would find similar results: Most people would be aware of what others are doing, yet unaware of what they themselves are doing to bring us to where we are today. This unawareness prevents us from seeing those forces in and outside of us that lead us to turn our differences into divides. These forces, summarized below and illustrated in these essays, are the invisible hand structuring the space between us.

As the list below suggests and these essays will show, we did not get to where we are today by any one path, but by many paths converging and moving us all in the same divisive direction. And while these forces affect different groups in different ways and to varying degrees, no group can escape their impact. Even those who call for greater inclusion, justice, and cooperation succumb to their influence. That is why civil rights leader Howard Thurman once asked: "What's the point of going to the promised land if you become the Pharaoh on your sojourn?"[27] and why novelist and philosopher Kwame Anthony Appiah cautioned: "Beware a group devoted to participatory democracy that is itself harshly autocratic."[28] No one is immune.

Figure 1.1: Forces That Turn Differences into Divides

- We all share a **history** in which groups were sorted and ranked according to their "innate characteristics."

- We all inherited from this history a set of **cultural beliefs** that lead us to think of groups more or less consciously in lesser-better, zero-sum terms.

- That history and culture together produced segmented, hierarchical **institutions** that shape the way we think and behave in and across groups.

- We all fall prey to **unconscious cognitive biases** that make it hard for us to see when we are making matters worse for ourselves or others.

- We all have **psychological defenses** that protect our identities, status, and self-esteem by ignoring or minimizing what we do to make matters worse.

Together, these forces are driving us closer to people like us and further away from those unlike us, increasing the divisiveness and polarization that is weakening our nation.

What happens when We the People become the problem?

Take a look at the graph below. Since 2000, political polarization in the U.S. has increased over two-fold, significantly more than any other "advanced" democracy.[29]

---

[27] Howard Thurman, *The Luminous Darkness* (Richmond, IN: Friends United Press, 2017, written in 1965).

[28] Kwame Anthony Appiah, "Liberation Psychology: How Frantz Fanon came to view violence as therapy," *New York Review,* February 24, 2022.

[29] Jennifer McCoy, Benjamin Press, Murat Somer, Ozlem Tuncel, "Reducing Pernicious Polarization: A Comparative Historical Analysis of Depolarization," Carnegie Endowment for International Peace, May 2022. Graph is from this article, which I have converted into black and white for this book.

Figure 1.2: Polarization in Advanced Democracies

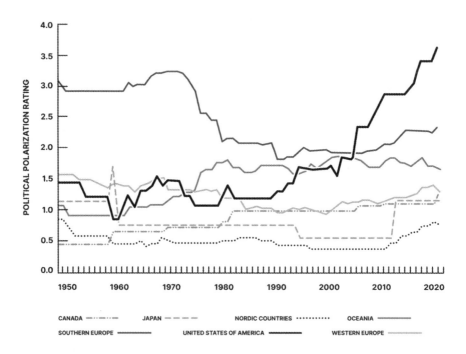

According to More in Common, 81 percent of Americans believe the resulting divisions pose a greater threat to our future than foreign nations.[30] That may be so, but foreign nations are taking full advantage. The Republican-led Senate Intelligence Committee during the Trump Administration concluded that Russian interference in the 2016 election was not so much designed to benefit one or another party as it was "part of a broader, sophisticated, and ongoing information warfare campaign designed to *sow discord in American politics and society . . . aimed at influencing how this nation's citizens think about themselves, their government, and their fellow Americans.*"[31]

That interference continues. Shortly before the 2022 midterm elections, the head of the Wagner paramilitary group in Russia, the late Yevgeny Prigozhin, bragged, "We have interfered, we are interfering, and we will continue to interfere—carefully, accurately, surgically and in our own way, as we know how to do."

[30] More in Common, "Exploring American Identity: Part 1."

[31] The Report of the Select Committee on Intelligence of the United States Senate on Russian Active Measures, Campaigns, and Interference in the 2016 U.S. Election, Volume 2: Russia's Use of Social Media, pp. 3–12. My emphasis.

He then added: "During our pinpoint operations, we will remove both kidneys and the liver at once."[32]

Efforts to increase our fear and loathing of one another feed off of political polarization, increasing civil unrest and decreasing trust. The risk intelligence company Verisk Maplecroft has twice downgraded our nation's risk profile to "high risk" since 2016, while a 2019 report from Pew Research Center reported a decline in trust.[33] "High levels of distrust make life uncomfortable, even difficult, and require extra measures for basic survival," says political scientist Dr. Danielle S. Allen. "In democracies that are marked by settled patterns of distrust, citizens develop modes of political behavior designed to maintain boundaries."[34] The more trust plummets, the thicker boundaries between groups grow and the more civil unrest rises.

Research by democracy expert Dr. Rachel Kleinfeld speaks to the cumulative impact on our democracy: "Democracies have primarily been dying at the hands of their own voters, who appreciate democracy but fear the other party so much that they will allow antidemocratic action to keep their side in power." That fear is putting us on one of the fastest downward trajectories of any democracy, says Kleinfeld, while rapidly narrowing our options for stopping it.[35] No longer are we the "city on the hill" to whom developing democracies look. We now sit among the world's flawed democracies, joining India, Brazil, and Indonesia.[36]

How We the People can become the solution

In 2017, historian Dr. Timothy Snyder took his meticulously researched book *Bloodlands,* an award-winning, 562-page account of Hitler and Stalin's mass killings, and distilled it into a 128-page guide on how to ward off tyranny. Among its twenty lessons from the twentieth century is an observation: "History permits us to be responsible, not for everything, but for something."[37]

[32] "Russia's Prigozhin admits interfering in U.S. elections," November 7, 2022. https://www.reuters.com/world/us/russias-prigozhin-admits-interfering-us-elections-2022-11-07/.

[33] Jimena Blanco, Karla Schiaffino, Victoria Gama, and Christian Wagner, "US named as 'high risk' country in new Civil Unrest Index," June 5, 2020; Lee Rainie and Andrew Perrin, "Key Findings about American's Trust in Government and Each Other," Pew Research Center, July 22, 2019. https://rb.gy/b3mjs.

[34] Danielle S. Allen, *Talking to Strangers: Anxieties of Citizenship since Brown v. Board of Education* (Chicago: University of Chicago, 2004), xix–xx.

[35] Rachel Kleinfeld, "Five Strategies to Support U.S. Democracy," Carnegie Endowment for International Peace, September 15, 2022, https://carnegieendowment.org/2022/09/15/five-strategies-to-support-u.s.-democracy-pub-87918.

[36] See the 2022 Democracy Index map is from *Economist Intelligence,* https://rb.gy/gnfld.

[37] Timothy Snyder, *On Tyranny: Twenty Lessons from the Twentieth Century* (New York: Tim Duggan Books, 2017), Kindle Ed., 125.

> **The most important "something" today is to shift from fighting against one another over past and present grievances to fighting with one another for a future that is better for all of us.**

I wrote these essays to help all of us, including me, shift from one to the other fight. The essays in Part 1 arm us for that fight, not with weapons but by building:

- A greater awareness of our history as a people and how it has shaped us all.

- An understanding of the new responsibilities that a multigroup democracy places on us.

- A renewed appreciation of the hopes and dreams we all bring to building a better future.

To create a better future and not simply repeat the past, it helps to understand how those who came before us created our past. As Snyder puts it, "History gives us the company of those who have done and suffered more than we have." In the doings and sufferings of those who came before us are invaluable lessons we can use to strengthen a multigroup democracy that is both enriched *and* challenged by its differences.

The essays in Parts 2 through 4 then turn to the present and future to tell stories of how citizens, online and offline, are working across groups in communities across our nation to resist forces of division and build a better future for all of us, not just some of us.

TWO

A
BRIEF HISTORY
of the
SPACE
BETWEEN US

On Independence Day in 2008, during a presidential campaign that raised the hopes of some and the fears of others, I marked the day in a small Vermont town snuggled between the Taconic and Green Mountain ranges. My husband and I were staying at an inn where our room shared a balcony with several others on the second floor. Early that morning, I took my coffee onto the balcony, where I found myself alone in one of several rocking chairs. The view in front of me was classic New England as far as the eye could see, with dozens of white clapboard buildings, their windows punctuated by black shutters, lined up in rows along quiet streets against a sage backdrop of mountains in the distance. A large American flag in front of the building moved lazily in a soft breeze off to my right. It was a rare moment of sublime peace, until I caught something flickering on the periphery of my vision. At first, I couldn't make out what it was, but then, as I turned toward the wall behind me, I saw a moving shadow, cast by the flag in the early sun. In that moment it struck me how even on the Fourth of July, this flag that signifies so much to so many about what is good in America could not escape its own shadow when the right light was cast upon it.

Many today see only the flag, many only its shadow. Those who created that flag did so in the pursuit of creating a better political system than the one they fled. Many of us today are seeking to create a better system than the one our

11

Founding Fathers and generations since have bequeathed to us. I figure, best we learn from that history, lest we repeat past mistakes or make even worse ones in our efforts to do better.

Our current system has its ideological roots in the earliest colonies of Jamestown, Virginia, and Plymouth, Massachusetts, the first giving rise to commerce at any cost, the latter to a deeply religious moral fervor rooted in Christianity. Both colonies and those that followed believed in and fought ferociously for unfettered freedom, autonomy, and independence, making governmental interference anathema to many, all the way up to today. These nascent forces, each of them powerful in their own right, were unstoppable together. They nurtured in the imagination of these early colonists a pragmatic, capitalist economic self-interest and a lofty set of democratic political ideals, the latter justifying and at times clashing with the former.

The Declaration of Independence grew out of this peculiar mix of forces. The slave trade was already well underway by then, as was the idea of race as a justification for enslaving Africans. In 1756, celebrated writer Voltaire captured the Zeitgeist of the so-called Age of Reason when he wrote in the pseudo-analytic language of the times: "The race of Negroes is a species of man different from our own in the same way that the breed of spaniels is different from that of greyhounds . . . one could say that if their intelligence is not of a different species from our own, it is far inferior." Voltaire was not alone or even the first to propagate such a belief. Fifteen years earlier in 1741, Bordeaux's Royal Academy of Sciences in France held a contest requesting that scholars submit papers on "the physical cause of the Negro's color, the quality of [the Negro's] hair, and the degeneration of both."[38]

By the time the Declaration was drafted, the assumption that Africans were lesser beings was a taken-for-granted "fact" among most White colonists, to be explored and explained, perhaps, but never questioned.[39] The vast majority of slave owners thought it entirely rational to deprive Africans of the same rights they claimed for themselves. Thomas Jefferson, who penned the words "all men are created equal" and who fathered six children with an enslaved household

[38] Henry Louis Gates Jr. and Andrew S. Curran, "Inventing the Science of Race," *New York Review,* December 16, 2021.

[39] My decision to capitalize both Black and White is based on APA's style rules and Kwame Anthony Appiah's reasoning laid out in the *Atlantic,* June 18, 2020. What's most important, as Appiah says, is that we "remember that black and white are both historically created racial identities—and avoid conventions that encourage us to forget this." See https://rb.gy/1hk8i.

servant, advanced the idea "as a suspicion only" that "blacks, whether originally a distinct race, or made distinct by time and circumstances, are inferior to the whites in the endowments both of body and mind."[40]

Jefferson's words come as no surprise to scholar Dr. Molefi Kete Asante who notes, "English Colonies of North America had experienced more than one hundred years of steady indoctrination in the legal idea that Africans were chattel and on the moral idea that Africans had no rights to life, liberty or the pursuit of happiness that Whites had to respect."[41] Annette Gordon-Reed, author of *The Hemingses of Monticello,* echoes Asante's interpretation. In an email to Gregory Schneider of the *Washington Post,* she wrote that the words Jefferson penned in the Declaration of Independence were inconsistent but not hollow. "He was born into a world that accepted monarchy, and all that went along with it—social hierarchy, wars brought on by disputes between royals, established churches that ran everyday people's lives. He thought the American Revolutionaries had created something 'new under the sun.'"[42]

Not everyone agreed. Abigail Adams, for one, voiced her objection to slavery in a letter to her husband, John Adams, four months before he signed the Declaration of Independence. "I have sometimes been ready to think," she wrote, "that the passion for Liberty cannot be Eaquelly [sic] Strong in the Breasts of those who have been accustomed to deprive their fellow Creatures of theirs." At the same time, enslaved and free African peoples living in Massachusetts petitioned the colonial government for their freedom, claiming it a natural right belonging to all men and women. Earlier, in 1739, Edward Oglethorpe fought the efforts of South Carolina merchants and land speculators to bring slavery to Georgia, arguing: "If we allow slaves we act against the very principles by which we associated together." Earlier still, German Quakers in Pennsylvania drafted a Petition Against Slavery in 1688 that proclaimed: "to bring men hither, or to rob and sell them against their will, we stand against. In Europe there are many oppressed for conscience sake; and here there are those oppressed who are of a black colour."[43]

Those who thought slavery a grievous sin and those who thought it a God-given institution made their arguments, signed petitions, wrote letters, appealed

[40] Thomas Jefferson, *Notes on the State of Virginia,* 1785. 2017.

[41] Dr. Molefi Kete Asante, "Slavery Remembrance Day memorial lecture 2007," https://rb.gy/onchhf.

[42] Gregory S. Schneider, "Jefferson's powerful last public letter reminds us what Independence Day is all about," *Washington Post,* July 3, 2017.

[43] Many made up the ranks of those opposing slavery; to name a few notables among them: Benjamin Lay, Olaudah Equiano, Anthony Benezet, Elizabeth Freeman, Benjamin Rush, and Moses Brown.

to religious doctrine, and cited scientific studies. *Yet the two groups remained so far apart in their beliefs and interests that neither could hear nor understand the other. With no resolution in sight, the practice of slavery raged on and grew ever more entrenched in the South's economy* until it became "the iconic capitalist venture of its era," as Dr. Asante put it. "If a European person was not in the game, he or she felt that they were missing out on an opportunity for great wealth. Given the strength of the idea that Africans were property, chattel, that could bring great wealth, some Europeans dubbed Africans, 'Black Gold.'"[44] Even though some Founders, like James Madison, rejected the idea that Africans were inferior and thought slavery a moral abomination, they stopped short of freeing their own slaves or fighting for slavery's eradication.[45]

Powerful forces and interests were at play, and they fueled a ferocious debate over race and slavery that continued up to and during the four-month-long Constitutional Convention held during one of the hottest, most humid summers Philadelphia had ever seen. By the time delegates convened in May 1787, close to 700,000 enslaved Africans were powering the fourth most lucrative economy in the world, and the burgeoning millionaire class in the South was not going to relinquish the institution without a fight. It was an asymmetrical negotiation. Those opposing slavery had little to offer their Southern brethren to get them to discard it, while Southerners could simply walk away and wreck the dream of an indivisible nation. After months of raucous wrangling, delegates from the South and North finally landed on a tortuous compromise: the Constitution would not stop or restrict slavery in the South, would add a fugitive slave clause requiring the return of escaped slaves, and would define slaves as three-fifths of a person when calculating state representation, in return for prohibiting slavery in the Northwest Territories and ending U.S. participation in the slave trade by 1808.

When forty-one of the original fifty-five delegates gathered on September 17 to sign or not to sign the final document, esteemed elder statesman Benjamin Franklin took center stage to address the frayed group. "There are several parts of this Constitution which I do not at present approve," he confessed, "but I am not sure I shall never approve them . . . (for) the older I grow, the more apt I am to doubt my own judgment, and to pay more respect to the judgment of others." With this object lesson in humility offered for the group's consideration, he continued:

---

[44] Asante, "Slavery Remembrance Day memorial lecture 2007."

[45] See Noah Feldman, "James Madison's Lessons in Racism," *New York Times,* October 28, 2017.

I doubt too whether any other Convention we can obtain may be able to make a better Constitution. For when you assemble a number of men to have the advantage of their joint wisdom, you inevitably assemble with those men, all their prejudices, their passions, their errors of opinion, their local interests, and their selfish views. From such an Assembly can a perfect product be expected? It therefore astonishes me, Sir, to find this system approaching so near to perfection as it does . . .

Those delegates who abhorred slavery, but loved their dream of a new nation more, acquiesced. It was a menacing dilemma, and it led to the first of many devil's bargains with race. In the end, they got a Constitution but at the price of legitimizing the idea that an innate hierarchy exists among groups, created by nature and sanctioned by God. The moment pen met paper, that idea was set free to flourish in our legal system, our economic structure, our culture, and our psyches, where it has survived a civil war, constitutional amendments, and civil rights legislation, despite the devastation it wrought then and has ever since.

In this history lies both our past damnation and our future salvation.

If ideas held by a group of powerful elites can enslave some of us and divide all of us, then new ideas created by a plurality of citizens can, in the same way, bring us together and set us all free.

THREE

OUR NATION IS CRUELLY TRAPPED

Erik Erikson, one of the bright lights of the twentieth century, was neither a historian, a political scientist, a cultural anthropologist, nor an economist. So I was surprised when he came to mind one morning while writing these essays. Erikson was a developmental psychologist with a deep interest in the interplay between the mind and society. His insights into how we develop—and the crises we face at each stage of development—have spanned time, countries, and generations. He is best known for coining the term "identity crisis," a crisis that usually emerges during our teenage years and sometimes persists beyond them. To resolve this crisis, we must answer the dual question of who we are and who we want to be. Should we fail, says Erikson, we will suffer role confusion, leaving us unable to commit to a coherent identity or a single path forward. By the time we become adults, if we have still not landed on a clear identity or path, we will struggle to make our way through future crises, with our lives growing more stagnant than generative. That is when I realized why Erikson had come to mind.

Our nation is "cruelly trapped," as James Baldwin put it, in a centuries-old identity crisis.[46] On five occasions, that crisis has erupted into prolonged periods of violence undertaken to define who we are and who we want to be once and for all, or at least for some. The first period involved a series of military campaigns to drive millions of Indigenous Peoples from their lands, so Americans of European descent could settle them. The second occurred when Southern plantation owners and Northern merchants built a system that systematically deployed violence

---

[46] From the documentary on James Baldwin, *I Am Not Your Negro* (2016).

16

to capture, transport, and enslave over ten million Africans for over two centuries.[47] The third took place when a four-year civil war took the lives of 620,000 soldiers to determine which would endure: our union or the institution of slavery.[48] The fourth emerged during and after Reconstruction, when Whites in the North and South, who believed in their innate superiority, used state-sanctioned violence to terrorize African Americans and strip them of their newly won constitutional rights.[49] The fifth occurred in the mid-twentieth century when White segregationists once again used state-sanctioned violence in an attempt to stop the Civil Rights Movement from reclaiming those Constitutional rights.

This quest of ours to define who we are and who we want to be has been a long, bloody road. Along the way, we have either contracted or expanded our definition of We the People, determining which groups have access to the rights and opportunities of the American dream and which do not. It is too early to say how we will settle our current crisis or whether it will lead to worsening violence. The only thing we can say for sure is this:

Neither war nor words have yet to resolve our identity crisis, trapping us in a chronic state of conflict that leaves us unprepared for and unequal to the demands of the twenty-first century.

So why is this? Why have neither war nor words succeeded in resolving our conflicts over who we are and who we want to be as a nation and as a people? The most potent cause is hidden in plain sight. The space between groups has never been close enough for us to create a lasting or coherent identity. The vast majority of us have always lived and continue to live separate lives divided along a litany of lines: racial, economic, geographic, cultural, and ideological, to name the most obvious.[50] These separate lives have always generated and continue to generate different and often diametrically opposed images, stories, myths, and visions of who we are and who we want to be. Few of us in any one group has

---

[47] J. David Hacker, "From '20. and odd' to 10 million: The growth of the slave population in the United States," *Slavery Abol.* 2020, 41(4): 840–855, https://pubmed.ncbi.nlm.nih.gov/33281246/.

[48] Data on the number of soldiers killed vary from 620,000 to 750,000. The number cited here can be found in "Civil War Casualties," American Battlefield Trust, https://rb.gy/zqn01.

[49] "Documenting Reconstruction Violence," (2020). Equal Justice Initiative. Violence also occurred in the Midwest and North.

[50] See Emily Richmond, "Schools Are More Segregated Today Than During the Late 1960s," *Atlantic,* June 11, 2012, and "Segregation in America: 'Dragging On and On,'" NPR's *Morning Edition*, February 18, 2011.

direct access or line of sight into how those in other groups live or experience life in America. Almost all of our cross-group insights are mediated by social media, twenty-four-hour cable news, oligarchs, or politicians, many of whom benefit from pushing us apart rather than bringing us together. As a result, those groups on one side of a divide cannot include in their definition of who we are and who we want to be the experiences of those on the other side, making all of our definitions woefully incomplete and often incompatible. Some of us see the flag, others only its shadow.

The rise of group identities and identity politics

In the absence of a national identity around which we can coalesce, group identities are rapidly solidifying as a defense against all the changes, uncertainties, and inequities that have proliferated over the past fifty years. While these solidified identities offer a sense of security and belonging in an unsure world, that sense of security and belonging comes at the price of blurring our identities as individuals. When a person's identity is either "white, or male, or a woman, or a Jew, or Black," civil rights strategist Eric K. Ward points out, "it strips them of the fullness of their humanity. It simply doesn't speak to who we are as humans." In what group or groups does the Black woman married to a White woman working at minimum wage in a rural county in the Midwest think she belongs? And in what group or groups would others put her in this categorical schema we use to sort and slot Americans by group? Wherever she is placed, it will simplify and distort who she is and who she is not, to which groups she belongs and to which she does not, who her people are and who her people are not. "Why is it that in the United States," asks historian Dr. Matthew Frye Jacobson, "a white woman can have black children but a black woman cannot have white children?"[51] No continuous categories here, only black-or-white, in-or-out choices, weighed and ranked differentially.

The same forces solidifying group identities are also pushing them further apart. On the economic front, those groups lower on the ladder are fighting more and more among themselves to secure a higher rung, while on the political front, those on the far right and left wings are battling it out daily over who should get cancelled and who should not.

Meanwhile, as these "lateral" groups squabble among themselves, those at the very top have been steadily increasing the "vertical" distance between them and

[51] Cited by Hua Hsu in "The End of White America?" *Atlantic,* January/February 2009.

everyone else, politically and economically. This has made it easier for them to impose their definition of America on everyone else—or at least to try. The relative success of their efforts may be why so few of us have noticed how many rural, working-class, White men have succumbed to opiate abuse, suicide, and extremism after decades battered by forces outside of their control. And that is likely why, until the murder of George Floyd, so many White people were unaware of the violence Black men face every time they step outside. ***What made these facts of American life invisible to so many, and what are we missing now?***

What James Baldwin said of his experience as a Black man in America might be said of any group systematically airbrushed out of the American dream: "It comes as a great shock to discover that the country which is your birthplace, and to which you owe your life and your identity, has not, in its whole system of reality, evolved any place for you."[52]

Baldwin speaks here to a third distance creating fissures within our identity: the "internal" distance between who we say we are and who we really are. It is to this distance that Baldwin referred when he said that we are cruelly trapped. It is also the one to which American abolitionist Frederick Douglass spoke a century before Baldwin when he said of his experience as a slave: "Your shouts of liberty and equality, hollow mockery; your prayers and hymns, your sermons and thanksgivings, with all your religious parade, and solemnity, are . . . a thin veil to cover up crimes which would disgrace a nation of savages."

> **As long as we maintain a gaping distance in our minds and in our realities among demographically and ideologically diverse groups and between who we say we are and who we really are, we will continue to create different images, subscribe to different narratives, and promote different identities as a nation: some of our flag, some of its shadow.**

Hannah Arendt once said that plurality is an essential aspect of the human condition and any system that does not face that fundamental social truth will fail. As Baldwin once said, people denied participation "by their very presence, will wreck it." That is especially true in a multigroup democracy like ours, comprised of groups who will no longer allow themselves to be elbowed out of the American Dream.

---

[52] See the U.S. government video in the documentary *I Am Not Your Negro* for the most compelling example.

As citizens, we face a choice

Today's multigroup reality confronts us with a choice: We can create an autocracy with a strong, unelected leader at its helm, as some on the far-right and far-left would prefer.[53] Or we can fight to impose one group's identity, beliefs, and interests on everyone else, tearing each other and the nation apart in the process. Or we can face our multigroup reality and use it to redefine ourselves as an interconnected, interdependent whole greater than any one of its parts.

Those who prefer the first option believe democracies are by their very nature too quarrelsome and sluggish. They require inefficient, time-consuming efforts to build consensus or to reach compromises across too many disparate and competing groups, producing more economic and political problems than they solve. As a result, they simply cannot keep up with twenty-first-century demands as quickly or as effectively as autocracies.

> **But our quarrelsome, sluggish, time-consuming inefficiencies as a multigroup democracy are not the problem. They are the consequence of a problem we can solve.**

The problem is the space between us. We remain so close within and so distant across groups that we cannot exercise the creative thought and cooperative behavior needed to move faster and respond smarter to the challenges we face. Conversely, if we do what tens of thousands of citizens are already doing, more and more of us will reach across divides to work on common problems in communities across the country. Out of the shared purpose and passion people bring to and derive from this work, a new multifaceted identity will gradually take shape, one that speaks to the dreams, values, and hopes of everyone who calls America their home.

The closer we get to achieving that vision, the more likely our multigroup democracy can meet the demands of the twenty-first century and free itself from an identity crisis that has trapped us since our founding.

---

[53] See, for example, Axios-Ipsos' September 2022 poll in Thor Benson, "The Uniquely American Future of US Authoritarianism," *Wired,* March 26, 2023. Also see Bloeser, Williams, Crawford and Harward's 2022 poll results in Beth Daley, "Large numbers of Americans want a strong, rough, anti-democratic leader" in *The Conversation.* February 7, 2023.

WE ARE ALL PRISONERS

and

WARDENS

In 1989, Derek Black was born into White nationalist "royalty." A smart kid and a quick study, by the time he was eleven years old, he had adopted and was already preaching the belief that Whites, under increasing threat from encroaching immigrants and Blacks, were entitled to enjoy the liberties of the United States unencumbered by other races. Living in West Palm Beach, just across the Lagoon from Donald Trump's compound at Mar-a-Lago, he went to school at home, taught by his father Don Black, a former leader of the Ku Klux Klan and the founder of Stormfront, the first major White supremacist site on the internet. Derek's godfather was the neo-Nazi David Duke, former grand wizard of the Ku Klux Klan and his mother's former husband. Derek's father cohosted a White nationalist radio show with Derek called the *Don and Derek Black* show, which aired weekly on a Florida-based radio station. This was Derek's first group, and it was as close and insular as a group can be.[54]

Years later, after attending college and disavowing White nationalism, Derek was interviewed by Krista Tippett, host of the podcast *On Being*. During the interview, he spoke of the "mental space" that makes closely knit, insular groups so closely knit and insular:

---

[54] For a superb account of Derek Black's transformation, see Eli Saslow, *Rising Out of Hatred: The Awakening of a Former White Nationalist* (Albany, NY: Anchor, 2019). I draw on this account throughout these essays.

Our motivation was much more focused on each other, other people within the movement itself, and going to events and seeing each other and reinforcing that "You believe this, and I believe this, and it's us against the world; and if we don't advocate this, no one else will." And *almost all the mental space* was devoted to that, trying to talk to other people who believe in the White nationalist ideology and reaffirm that we're in this together. And *very little mental space* was actually spent on anybody else and even worrying if what we're advocating has a negative impact on anyone else, because we were so convinced that it was right, for us and for the world, and *there was no possibility that that wasn't true.*[55]

In his 1885 memoir, Ulysses S. Grant recounts how this same self-affirming mode of thought, enclosed in a tight mental space, led poor Whites in the South to support a war for slavery that was not in their interest:

The great bulk of the legal voters of the South were men who owned no slaves; their homes were generally in the hills and poor country; their facilities for educating their children even up to the point of reading and writing were very limited; their interest in the contest was very meagre—what [interest] there was, if they were capable of seeing it, was with the North; they too needed emancipation. Under the old regime they were looked down upon by those who controlled all the affairs in the interests of slaveowners, as poor white trash who were allowed the ballot so long as they cast it according to direction . . . The shot-gun was not resorted to. Masked men did not ride over the country at night intimidating voters; but *there was a firm feeling that a class existed in every State with a sort of divine right to control public affairs. If they could not get this control by one means they must by another. The end justified the means. The coercion, if mild, was complete.*[56]

What U.S. President Grant learned about pre–Civil War America, many before and since have used to get and keep power: it doesn't require terror, threats, or laws to impose control when the people you want to control live and think in a closed mental space and share the same firm feeling.

More than 150 years later, scholar Dr. Dale Craig Tatum describes how Donald Trump implemented a "racial wedge strategy" to win the presidency by catering to disillusioned Whites pummeled by forces outside their control.[57] It was

---

[55] "How Friendships and Quiet Conversations Transformed a White Nationalist," *On Being,* May 17, 2018. My emphasis. https://rb.gy/k3lq9g.

[56] Ulysses S. Grant, *Personal Memoirs of Ulysses S. Grant* (Pittsburgh, PA: General Press, 2022), Kindle Ed., 173. My emphasis.

[57] Dale Craig Tatum, "Donald Trump and the Legacy of Bacon's Rebellion," *Journal of Black Studies,* 2017, 651–674.

a tried-and-true strategy used many times before in our nation's history. As far back as 1676 in Jamestown, Virginia, land-owning colonials deployed the strategy after a coalition of indentured Black and White servants and Native Americans led by Nathaniel Bacon burned Jamestown to the ground during Bacon's Rebellion.[58] As soon as the ash settled, colonial elites rushed to pass laws to stop the alliance from ever reassembling by turning African colonists into hereditary slaves, driving Native Americans from their lands, and giving White indentured servants new freedoms and greater status. For the first time, the words *white* and *black* in reference to race trickled into public documents and private papers, distinguishing European colonists from those of African descent.

These changes in law and lexicon—the one formal, the other informal—combined to create what Dr. Tatum calls an "illusion of inclusion" among poor Whites. It was a powerful illusion, so powerful that it led unprivileged Whites to move closer politically and psychologically to privileged Whites who cared nothing for their interests, and further away from people of color with whom they shared an abiding interest in greater freedom and equality.[59]

The staying power of a discredited belief

Over the past three decades, the belief in an innate hierarchy has regained strength, much like a hurricane moving over warm water with too little wind shear to stop it. With help from a few far-right billionaires and the politicians wooing them, ideologies about one or another group's inferiority or superiority have been steadily pushing their way back into mainstream and social media. In the *HuffPost* in August 2023, Christopher Mathias uncovered that conservative writer Richard Hanania used to write under the pseudonym Hoste as a self-proclaimed "race realist."[60] A few days later, in the Substack newsletter *The Racket*, journalist Jonathan M. Katz cited a post in which Hanania (as Hoste) wrote:

> "There doesn't seem to be a way to deal with low IQ breeding that doesn't include coercion. . . . In the same way we lock up criminals and the mentally ill in the interests of society at large, one could argue that we could on the exact same

---

[58] See Erin Blakemore, "Why America's First Colonial Rebels Burned Jamestown to the Ground," *History*, https://rb.gy/w3qdxi. Little known fact: Bacon organized the coalition in a cynical effort to drive Native Americans from land he coveted.

[59] Tatum, "Donald Trump and the Legacy of Bacon's Rebellion."

[60] Christopher Mathias, "Richard Hanania, Rising Right-Wing Star, Wrote For White Supremacist Sites Under Pseudonym," HuffPost, August 4, 2023.

principle sterilize those who are bound to harm future generations through giving birth."

According to Katz, Hanania was proposing to sterilize anyone with IQs less than ninety, adding: "In case there is any doubt about who he was referring to, a few years earlier Hanania called Black people 'a race with an IQ of 85.' Latinos, he added, also don't have 'the requisite IQ to be a productive part of a first world nation.'"[61]

In August 2023, Hanania renounced his Hoste persona and recanted his views in the online magazine *Quillette*. "Phrases like 'racism' and 'misogyny' get thrown around too easily," wrote Hanania, "but I don't believe there's any doubt many of my previous comments crossed the line, regardless of where one thinks that line should be. . . . So yes, I truly sucked back then." Since then, Hanania says, he has come to see differences among groups, well, differently: "Other writers have shifted my views on specific issues. Bryan Caplan and Alex Nowrasteh have convincingly argued that even if groups differ in skills or cognitive abilities, we can all still benefit from the division of labor."[62] I cannot help but wonder who he has in mind for doing what labor.

New York Magazine staff writer, Zak Cheney-Rice, captured the essence of the shift: "The New Hanania leaves out the first part—'the sources of such disparities'—while heaping blame on Black people for their problems and calling for aggressive action. On May 13, he tweeted, 'We need more policing, incarceration, and surveillance of black people. Blacks won't appreciate it, whites don't have the stomach for it.'"[63]

As Cheney-Rice points out, nowhere in his confessional does Hanania disavow his causal theories about innate differences despite decades of scholarship that disconfirm them:

> [Hanania's] laboratory for proving this theory, Chicago, is a source of some of the richest scholarship available on the subject of residential segregation and its relationship to crime. The work of historians like Arnold Hirsch and Beryl Satter, along with that of sociologists Douglas Massey and Nancy Denton, details how the city's white residents and political and financial institutions transformed formerly white neighborhoods into Black ghettos through the early-to-mid-20th

[61] Jonathan M. Katz, "Hanania's defense," *Racket,* August 8, 2023.

[62] Richard Hanania, "My Journey Out of Extremism," *Quillette,* August 7, 2023.

[63] Zak Cheney-Rice, "Our Journey Into Extremism: The revealing case of the anti-woke crusader Richard Hanania," *New York Magazine,* August 12, 2023.

century. . . . As the borders of these neighborhoods hardened and they became overcrowded and physically degraded, one result was a concentration of poverty's ills, like joblessness, homelessness, addiction, and crime . . ."[64]

Hanania's recent book, *The Origins of Woke,* garnered glowing praise from Silicon Valley billionaire Peter Theil. "D.E.I. will never d-i-e from words alone," wrote Theil. "Hanania shows we need the sticks and stones of government violence to exorcise the diversity demon." Chiming in, Republican presidential candidate Vivek Ramaswamy lauded the book for delivering "a devastating kill shot to the intellectual foundations of identity politics in America." I cannot help but wonder just whose violence we ought to fear.

On the heels of Hanania's *Quillette* article, journalist Jamelle Bouie took up the question of how a discredited seventeenth-century belief could regain strength in the twenty-first century. "If some groups are simply meant to be at the bottom," Bouie suggests, "then there are no questions to ask about their deprivation, isolation and poverty. There are no questions to ask about the society which *produces* that deprivation, isolation and poverty. And there is nothing to be done, because nothing can be done: *Those people are just the way they are.*"[65]

In other words, the belief persists because it serves the few who have the most, even if it harms the many who have much less. And that raises another question:

> **Why are so many of us letting an old idea regain strength? Why are we not acting like the wind shear that stops hurricanes from restrengthening over warm waters?**

Toni Morrison's account of struggling European immigrants coming to America suggests one answer: "Wherever they were from, they would stand together," she wrote. "They could all say, 'I am not [Black]'. . . It wasn't negative to them—it was unifying. When they got off the boat, the second word they learned was '[n----r].' Every immigrant knew he would not come at the very bottom. He had to come above at least one group—and that was us."[66]

No one wants to be at the very bottom; all of us aspire to move up in the world; some of us won't rest until we are at the very top. But this archaic belief

---

[64] Ibid.

[65] Jamelle Bouie, "Why an Unremarkable Racist Enjoyed the Backing of Billionaires," *New York Times,* August 12, 2023. My emphasis.

[66] Cited by Tatum. From Angelo, 1989, p. 120.

that there is an innate racial hierarchy based on God's will or nature's design is nothing more than a quirk of our in-group/out-group evolutionary heritage, a vestige of the aristocratic thinking our Founders both fled and brought with them from monarchist Europe.

Yet in its heyday, this belief was so powerful that it spawned and justified not only slavery, but one caste-based, hierarchical institution after another, from our schools to our workplaces to our courts to our churches and beyond.[67] To this day, those institutions structure our everyday experience in light of this vestigial belief, embedding it so deeply in our psyches and in our culture that we are still vulnerable to it.

Few politicians appreciated this fact of American life more than President Lyndon Johnson. His rise to power early in his career was built on exploiting it. While traveling across the South with Bill Moyers, a young staffer at the time, Johnson reflected on how the racial-wedge strategy works in practice. Moyers recounts:

> We were in Tennessee. During the motorcade, he spotted some ugly racial epithets scrawled on signs. Late that night in the hotel, when the local dignitaries had finished the last bottles of bourbon and branch water and departed, he started talking about those signs.

> "I'll tell you what's at the bottom of it," he said. "If you can convince the lowest white man he's better than the best colored man, he won't notice you're picking his pocket. Hell, give him somebody to look down on, and he'll empty his pockets for you."[68]

Losing our footing as a society

In his book *Dying of Whiteness*, Dr. Jonathan Metzl tells the story of Trevor, a forty-one-year-old White man dying of liver disease in Tennessee, a thirty-nine-minute car ride from Kentucky. In Kentucky, Trevor would have been a top candidate to receive lifesaving medications or even a transplant, because Kentucky had adopted the expansion of Medicaid under the Affordable Care Act. In Tennessee, where elected officials had repeatedly blocked "Obamacare" reforms, Trevor would be left to die untreated. That was fine by Trevor. "Ain't no way I would ever support Obamacare or sign up for it," he told Metzl. "I would rather die . . . no way I want my tax dollars paying for Mexicans or welfare queens." Like many

---

[67] For a comprehensive exploration of how our society is shaped by a hidden caste system, see Isabel Wilkerson's superb book, *Caste: The Origins of Our Discontents* (New York: Random House, 2020).

[68] Bill Moyers, "What a Real President Was Like," *Washington Post*, November 13, 1988.

others whose identities, status, and economic well-being had been whittled away by forces outside their control, Trevor sought refuge in the only place he could find it: his belief in a racial hierarchy. There, he could claim his "rightful" place and salvage one last smidgeon of self-respect before dying, poor and alone.

The official medical cause given for Trevor's death was liver disease brought on by the toxic effects of a lifetime of drinking. But Dr. Metzl thought that diagnosis incomplete: "I could not help but think that Trevor's deteriorating condition resulted also from the toxic effects of dogma [that] aligned with beliefs about a racial hierarchy that overtly and implicitly aimed to keep white Americans hovering above Mexicans, welfare queens, and other nonwhite others."[69] Trevor would die to keep "his place in this hierarchy, rather than participate in a system that might put him on the same plane as immigrants or racial minorities."

Trevor is far from alone. In-depth research conducted by Dr. Metzl over six years in the Midwest and the South reveals how our cultural belief in a racial hierarchy is not only killing people of color, which we have long known, but large swaths of White people as well.[70] And not only our health and mortality are at stake. In her bestselling book *The Sum of Us*, Heather McGhee documents in exquisite detail how this belief is causing our society as a whole to lose its footing: "the antiquated belief that some groups of people are better than others distorts our politics, drains our economy, and erodes everything Americans have in common, from our schools to our air to our infrastructure."[71]

Putting a vestigial belief to rest

In an age light on facts and heavy on furor, even documentation as thorough as McGhee's and Metzl's runs the risk of falling on deaf ears. Empirical arguments for or against any belief rarely convince the other side. If anything, the resulting two-sided debates over which side is factually right or wrong only lock each side in further.[72] An alternative, then, might be to ask:

> **What kind of society will a belief create if people act upon it as if it is true, and is that the kind of society we want?**

[69] Jonathan Metzl, *Dying of Whiteness: How the Politics of Racial Resentment Is Killing America's Heartland* (New York: Basic Books, 2019).

[70] Also see Nancy Krieger et al., "Relationship of political ideology of US federal and state elected officials and key COVID pandemic outcomes following vaccine rollout to adults: April 2021–March 2022," *Lancet Regional Health*, https://rb.gy/ntjg3r.

[71] Heather McGhee, *The Sum of Us* (New York: One World, 2021), Kindle Ed., 17.

[72] See Essay 8: "Wedded to Conflict for Better and for Worse."

When people in recent human history have acted collectively upon the belief that some groups are innately inferior, they have created societies that promoted slavery, restricted the individual rights and freedoms of groups deemed inferior, and committed genocide to cull the human herd of them. Are these really the kinds of societies we want?

In a pluralist world, in which it is increasingly difficult and dangerous for one group to unilaterally impose its interests on another, the belief in an innate hierarchy has outlived its sell-by date. It is now rotting on the shelf where some continue to sell it and many continue to buy it. It sits there still because those who came before us passed the belief down to us through institutions built upon it, and then we bought it without giving it much, if any, thought. And herein lies an overlooked conundrum we cannot solve until we look it square in the face:

> **On the one hand, these institutions shape who we are, how we think, and what we do. On the other hand, who we are, how we think, and what we do shape these institutions.**

All of us are prisoners *and* wardens of these institutions. What Václav Havel once said of a post-totalitarian communist state, we can also say of our struggling democracy: by accepting the rules of the game, we become players in the game, making it possible for the game to go on.[73] That means no matter how often our institutions may disappoint us, we cannot create new ones until you and I revisit and revise two tightly linked beliefs upon which these institutions rest:

- Some groups are innately better or lesser than others, making members of those groups more or less deserving of and entitled to opportunities and resources.

- One group's gain must come at another's expense; for one group to win, another group must lose.

Until we put these vestigial beliefs out of *our* misery, our institutions will continue to breed alienation and mistrust until they fail altogether. The basic problem is this: any system in which the interests of a few prevail over the interests of many—who out of fear, despair, or indifference accept it—is inherently unstable and will, at some point, crumble like a building too weak to withstand its own

---

[73] Václav Havel, *The Power of the Powerless,* (Abingdon-on-Thames, Oxfordshire, UK: Routledge, 2016), Kindle Ed., 31 and 36.

weight. Hence, the rise and fall of tribes, countries, and empires, one after another, spanning history in an endless game of deadly dominoes.

Today, we all rise and fall together, coexisting as we do in an interconnected space that is no longer expanding but shrinking. A virus in China now travels the globe in weeks, shattering lives and shuttering businesses, while the smoke from trees in the Amazon, burned to profit a few, chokes us all. The earth and its peoples used to forgive us such lapses, but no longer:[74]

> **Our zero-sum mindset and win-lose competitive zeal, bolstered by outdated beliefs, is fast exhausting our planet's resources, our resilience as a nation, and our spirit as a people.**

Our survival, as a nation and as a planet, depends on our cultivating within ourselves and each other the self-awareness and mutual responsibility needed to restructure not only our formal laws and policies but our beliefs, our institutions, and the space between us to enable and encourage greater cooperation across groups. It is in all of our interests that we do so.

According to political philosopher Alan Coffee, Frederick Douglass made a similar point, both before and after the Civil War:

> Douglass argues that the only sustainable way to avoid a damaging confrontation is by rigorously overhauling how social groups interact with each other. A thorough restructuring is necessary; otherwise, one generation might be reconciled, only to have the social system that gave rise to the division reemerge in the next. . . . Crucially, Douglass emphasizes, alongside economic and political reforms there must be a cultural reformation in which the national stories, reference points and sense of identity are reevaluated and renewed collaboratively with all sections of society participating.[75]

Now that a "damaging confrontation" once again looms, perhaps we are more ready to listen.

---

[74] My thanks to Dr. David Diamond, psychoanalyst and literary critic, whose comments I build on here.

[75] Alan Coffee, "150 years ago, Frederick Douglass predicted the United States' dilemma today," *Washington Post*, August 6, 2021.

FIVE

THE LOCKED MIND

We have long understood that our minds navigate the complexity of everyday life by putting things, events, and people into categories. In the blink of an eye, we move from observing people or groups to interpreting them to deciding how to respond. Forget Malcolm Gladwell's ten thousand hours to mastery.[76] From the moment we are born, we spend *millions* of hours swishing up what Chris Argyris and Don Schön first called a "ladder of inference," moving from one or more facts to our conclusions about what those facts mean, using well-worn categories to pave the way. Before long, we lose sight of the steps we took to reach our conclusions and see only the constructs in our heads, not the multifaceted people or groups out there in reality.

Worse, once we sort and slot people into some category—liberals, elites, deplorables, Black activists, White supremacists, socialists—we no longer *want* to see them; we no longer *want* to get to know them. In our minds, they have become what writer E.M. Forster calls "flat characters," two-dimensional stereotypes whose contexts, motives, hurts, and longings are irrelevant. Their function is purely to play a role in our own narrative, drowning out the curiosity and courage needed to reach across the space between us. Why would we do it? There's nothing there but a bunch of flat characters, most of them villains, some of them out to get us. People in our own group, by contrast, are close enough for us to get to know them, to flesh them out, to see them more fully. They become what Forster calls "round characters," complex people whose inner lives and outer circumstance are available to our eye. We can see what they see, feel what they feel, and think what they think. From that up-close perspective, they appear in our minds as mostly rational, well-intended, good people, up against a lot, working hard to create a better world for themselves and their families, and making a good number of sacrifices to do it.

---

[76] Malcolm Gladwell, *Outliers: The Story of Success*. (New York, NY: Back Bay Books, 2001.

New York Times columnist David Brooks wisely suggests that we inoculate against the dangers of categorizing people and groups by acknowledging that all such categories are wrong, even hurtful to some degree. "We should be much more suspicious of our categories, much quicker to acknowledge that they are sometimes helpful but always simplistic fabrications." That makes so much sense, you have to wonder, *Why don't more of us do it?*—because clearly few of us do. The vast majority of us believe so much in the categories we impose on others that it would never occur to us to give them a moment's thought. ***The only suspiciousness we demonstrate toward categories is for those that others impose on us.***

Listen to what former White nationalist Derek Black says to *On Being* host Krista Tippett when she asks if he would have labeled the White nationalist internet site Stormfront a hate site when he was still involved in the movement:

> Oh, no. No, in the same way that the community would never use the word "racist"; they would say, absolutely not "racist," because that means "bad person," and we're not "bad people." We don't "hate," and we don't "dislike"; we're just interested in "preserving our own." That sort of language would never happen within the movement itself . . . No; no, it was purely in the sense that there is an opposition in mainstream society to this clearly biologically true and correct, and socially correct ideology, and so they come up with insults like the word "racist," and "hate." And the job of an activist is to sidestep and point out the hypocrisy of them using this word, "hate." *And it's not something that people attribute to themselves or think that others are correct to use it.* [77]

What Derek says of the White nationalist community might be said of all groups. None of us see ourselves as others do, because we all see ourselves from *the inside out,* not from *the outside in,* as others see us. It is a well-documented but largely unrecognized quirk of our minds and our defenses. While we can easily see what others are doing and how that affects us, we cannot as easily see—nor do most of us want to see—what we are doing and how that affects others.

If ever there was a surefire way to cultivate empathy within groups and animosity across groups, this is it. If people in groups can only see what they are feeling and what other groups are doing to trigger those feelings, but do not see what they are doing to trigger negative reactions in other groups, everyone across groups will quite naturally blame one another for making their lives a living hell with nary a backward glance at themselves. With no one any the wiser, the distance within groups draws ever closer and the distance across groups ever wider.

> **These mental quirks—slotting and sorting, flattening and rounding, seeing others' roles but not our own—all conspire to maintain the space between us.**

Freeing one another from these mental traps will allow us to access our collective intelligence and use it to build a better future. Social psychologist Jonathan Haidt says the most common obstacle to good thinking is confirmation bias, the tendency to see and search only for evidence that confirms our beliefs. The most reliable cure, says Haidt, is interaction with people who don't share your beliefs: "People who think differently and are willing to speak up if they disagree with you make you smarter, almost as if they are extensions of your own brain."[78] If ever we needed help extending our brains, it is now.

---

[78] Jonathan Haidt, "Why the Past 10 Years of American Life Have Been Uniquely Stupid," *Atlantic,* April 11, 2022.

SIX

CULTURE'S THUMBPRINT

In 1998, psychologists Drs. Mahzarin Banaji, Tony Greenwald, and Brian Nosek devised a test called the Implicit Association Test, or IAT, to measure the associations we make out of our experience in the social world. Early on, those taking one of their most popular tests—the racial bias test—were stunned to discover that they were quicker to associate the faces of Black people with unpleasant words and the faces of White people with pleasant ones.[79] Many grew defensive. "Your test is stupid," they would write the IAT team. "I do not have a race bias. I am a rap musician. How dare you tell me I am biased."[80] Yet the results were irrefutable, backed up by millions of tests taken around the world.

"Harm is happening without the person doing the harm being aware they're doing it," says Dr. Mahzarin Banaji of the results. "What does that mean for the big question of how we are going to treat each other in a democratic society where we believe in fairness?"[81]

Our evolutionary legacy at work

From early memory studies, psychologists have long known that when two things repeatedly occur together—bacon and eggs, salt and pepper, mother and father—they forge a strong connection in our minds. "What's wired together fires together," quip neuroscientists. To find out how strongly what fires together is wired together in the social world, the IAT team drew on computer-aided brain

---

[79] "Can we unlearn implicit biases? With Mahzarin Banaji, PhD." *Speaking of Psychology*, Episode 199, July 13, 2022. This section is based on this interview with Dr. Banaji, which I paraphrased and edited for clarity.

[80] Ibid.

[81] Ibid.

science to first build and then post on their website a series of tests, measuring the associations people make around gender, race, sexuality, and so on.

In the first month alone, 45,000 people visited their website to complete one or another test. Today, more than 20 million people have taken an IAT, creating an unparalleled longitudinal database.[82] The team now has data from countries around the world and from every county in the United States, collected every second of the day and night. Among those most astounded by the quality and quantity of the data is Dr. Banaji herself: "You can look at elderly people, young people, people who live on the coast, in the middle of the country, the north, the south, the rich, the poor, the educated, the less educated. You can look at any of these."

The people taking the tests cannot believe their eyes. They go into it assuming that their conscious beliefs in fairness, equality, and justice will spare them from bias. They come out discovering that these conscious beliefs cannot inoculate them against a lifetime of experience in cultures that put things together differently.

Table 6.1: Racial Bias Implicit Association Test (IAT)

Implicit Association Test

Next, you will use the 'E' and 'I' computer keys to categorize items into groups as fast as you can. These are the four groups and the items that belong to each:

Category	Items
Good	Happy, Joyful, Delight, Excellent, Friend, Terrific, Glorious, Attractive
Bad	Hurtful, Failure, Angry, Evil, Rotten, Annoy, Bothersome, Scorn
Black people	
White people	

There are seven parts. The instructions change for each part. Pay attention!

Continue

Source: Racial Bias Test on Project Implicit Website

In all of these data, Dr. Banaji sees our evolutionary legacy. "We carry in our minds the vestiges of a time and a place in our history where we lived with people

---

[82] Project Implicit Website: https://implicit.harvard.edu/implicit/user/jaxt/blogposts/piblogpost020.html.

who were just like us in our own little tribe. On the other side of the mountain was another group of people who looked different from us even though we were genetically the same. Maybe they put a different mark on their face or wore a different kind of clothing. And so when we met over some resource like food or water, we learned to do some not-very-nice things to those other people in order to survive."[83]

Our society, like all societies, has built upon this evolutionary legacy a set of more or less implicitly held cultural beliefs about the innate value of different groups.[84] So deeply embedded are these beliefs today that Dr. Banaji's own personal IAT results associated women with the home. Neither a mother working outside the home nor her own illustrious career were enough to counter the effects of her early immersion in a culture in South India where most women stayed home. Findings like this, replicated again and again, eventually led Dr. Banaji to refer to implicit bias as "the thumbprint of our culture on our brain." When asked if this thumbprint can be changed, Dr. Banaji is unequivocal:

> **"Of course it can be changed. Because it was learned, you can make yourself unlearn it. The mistake people make is to think that they can unlearn it easily."**

Research undertaken by Dr. Tessa Charlesworth, a postdoc working with Dr. Banaji, underscores the challenge. She wanted to know how six biases had changed, if at all, between 2007 and 2020: racial bias, skin-tone bias, anti-gay bias, and biases against overweight people, old people, and the disabled. Although she found a notable decrease in three of the six biases—anti-gay bias (64 percent), racial bias (26 percent), and skin-tone bias (25 percent)—she also uncovered a disturbing gap. While implicit racial and skin-tone bias had decreased by 26 and 25 percent respectively, people's conscious (explicit) racial bias had decreased an astronomical 98 percent, creating over a 70 percent gap between our conscious beliefs and our implicit biases.[85]

That gap is now wreaking havoc. With a 98 percent change in people's conscious beliefs, many people assume that they are no longer biased, while the

---

[83] Ibid.

[84] See Essay 4: "We Are All Prisoners and Wardens."

[85] Tessa E.S. Charlesworth and Mahzarin R. Banaji, "Patterns of Implicit and Explicit Attitudes: IV. Change and Stability From 2007 to 2020, *Psychological Science,* vol. 33, no. 9 (2022): 1347–1371. https://doi.org/10.1177/09567976221084257.

persistence of implicit bias leads those bearing the brunt of racial bias to see relatively little change.

Closing the gap and unlocking its Catch-22

Given the damage wreaked by unconscious racial bias, Banaji and her team tested three interventions to see which, if any, might reduce it. In the first intervention, the team told subjects to treat groups equally without any bias; it had no effect at all. In the second, they exposed subjects to new associations—pairing Black faces with good things, White faces with less good things—to see if new associations could replace old ones. It produced only slightly better results. In the third, they asked subjects to imagine themselves suffering in some way and then to imagine a Black person helping them while a White person did not. This produced the biggest change, but it quickly wore off as people's "brains snapped back," once they returned to the real world, where they saw the same old associations between Black and bad, White and good.

So what will it take to reduce implicit racial bias and close the gap? Dr. Banaji found the seeds of an idea in how fast and how far anti-gay bias decreased. She suspects that when gay people began to "come out" in larger and larger numbers, it created intense "cognitive dissonance" among families and friends between their anti-gay beliefs and their love for the person who just said they were gay. To resolve this conflict, they had to either change their belief or sever their relationship with a loved one. "People went with love," says Dr. Banaji. "The love of a child, or the love of a neighbor or a friend trumped the belief."

When it comes to racial bias, however, things are not quite so simple. Banaji points out:

> The two domains in which we live are home and work. In both domains, we are deeply segregated by race. We just don't see people across lines of race. So the chance that you would . . . have the same kind of experience that straight parents and straight grandparents had to deal with when the time came is just not an opportunity that race offers us.

This fact of American life led Dr. Banaji to ask a question that cannot be answered in her lab because it can only be answered by us: ***"As a society, what will we do about this degree of segregation if we care about racial bias?"*** Any answer to that question will have to address a thorny Catch-22 suggested by the IAT:

- Widespread implicit bias will only change when more of us see and experience new associations in the real world.

- But we cannot see or experience new associations in the real world as long as our implicit biases keep us segregated and our segregated reality keeps us biased.

One way around this Catch-22 is to draw on our conscious beliefs to make a conscious choice to cross the divides that separate us, as the stories in Parts 2 through 4 illustrate. The people in each of these stories:

- Opened the mental space within their own racial groups by inviting challenge, seeking out new ideas, perspectives, and facts, and exploring their implicit biases.

- Worked on common problems across racial groups, creating the positive associations needed to transform implicit biases.

One thing Charlesworth's data made clear: changing implicit biases will likely go further faster if we stop simply telling people not to be biased (recall, telling had no effect), and if we instead help each other in and across groups to see biases we cannot see in ourselves but can see in others (recall, helping had the biggest effect). As Part 3 illustrates in detail, a little help from our cross-group friends can go a long way toward creating a different kind of real world.

SEVEN

WHERE OUR RESPONSIBILITY LIES

The U.S. Constitution guarantees We the People innumerable rights: those in the original Bill of Rights plus later amendments passed to expand those rights. In return, we are obliged to do only four things: obey the law, pay taxes, serve on juries, and register with the Selective Service. Beyond that, our responsibilities are pretty much up to us, including whether to stay informed or to vote. Nowhere in formal documents or informal custom are we expected to do anything else.

Fast-forward 232 years since the Bill of Rights was ratified, and We the People are the problem. As Bulwark editor Jonathan V. Last points out, many of our current political woes spring not only from big money but from small-dollar donors, more and more of whom are fueling the ascendancy of candidates that range anywhere from poor to downright dangerous. This is to be expected, says Last: "You cannot expect normal people to have considered opinions about complex issues such as the debt ceiling or immigration policy, or the war in Ukraine. Normal people have lives; they don't read a lot of news. It's not fair to expect them to be well informed."[86]

Fair enough, though *perhaps it is expecting so little of so many for so long that has brought us to where we are today.* Much education and psychological research shows that you get from people what you expect of people, with higher expectations leading to higher performance and lower expectations leading to lower performance.[87] Since our democratic system depends so much on We the

---

[86] Jonathan V. Last, "The People Are the Problem," *The Triad,* May 5, 2023.

[87] Jose Eos Trinidad, "Collective Expectations Protecting and Preventing Academic Achievement," *Education and Urban Society,* vol. 51, no. 9 (2019): 1147–71; C.E. Sanders, T.M. Field, M.A. Diego, "Adolescents' academic expectations and achievement," *Adolescence,* vol. 36, no. 144 (2001): 795–802.

People, and We the People are the problem, perhaps it is time we started expecting more of ourselves—or else, as Last says, "Good luck, America."

How did our Founders' solution become the problem?

As citizens, we quite rightly expect our government to solve common problems, while minding its own business and staying out of ours. We quite wrongly expect very little of ourselves. In his 1961 inaugural address, President John F. Kennedy became the first and last peacetime president to challenge us to "ask not what your country can do for you, but what you can do for your country." Apparently he thought we needed reminding.

So where does this asymmetry between what we expect of our leaders, our institutions, and our government and what we expect of ourselves as citizens come from? One answer lies in our history and in the informal system of expectations that history produced.

We are a nation forged by a war of independence, fought against governmental tyranny, and built on the value of individual rights, unequally applied and unevenly justified. We have built upon this founding DNA a nation of highly independent, differentially treated groups with more rights than responsibilities and more fights than filial attachments. In families, those conditions are known to produce spoiled brats, intent on besting one another and getting their own way rather than having each other's backs or challenging one another to do better, to be better.

Small wonder that when fights break out today over how best to solve a problem, many groups look to our government to settle the issue in their favor, like squabbling siblings look to their parents. Some groups—among them, White nationalists, far-right extremists, and the disaffected superrich—act like favored children fearful of losing their historic "fair share" of the goods. Like those favored children, they complain vociferously when politicians or policies do not win for them everything to which they have come to feel entitled. Outraged by the "injustice," they attack not just the policies and politicians, but the motives, character, and integrity of our government and the sanity and morality of the groups they think are holding it hostage. It would never occur to them that if there is a swamp in Washington, they had a hand in creating it.

Our Founders would be dismayed, though perhaps not surprised. They fled monarchist Europe to build a nation of the people, by the people, and for the people, even if "the people" they had in mind at the time was a single homogeneous group of White men. They established that democracy in a world that took months to traverse, on a continent seemingly without end, overflowing with natural resources, protected by oceans on two sides; populated by a diverse and dispersed network of Indigenous Peoples overcome and nearly wiped out by violence, disease, and sheer numbers; their wealth fueled by Africans who, regarded and treated as chattel, all but eliminated the cost of labor.

Our Founders did not and could not anticipate a world that takes only hours to traverse by air, milliseconds to span by technology, on a continent with porous borders and too few resources to meet unquenchable demand, populated by diverse groups with conflicting needs and interests who shall not be overcome or appeased.

Where do we go from here?

So where does a multigroup democracy go from here? We may be among the oldest constitutional democracies, but as a multigroup democracy, we are still quite young. Only since the 1965 Voting Rights Act have we included at the electoral table the full array of demographically diverse groups living in the U.S.[88] "The crossroads that American democracy is at right now are pretty damn close to unique," Harvard government professor Dr. Steven Levitsky said during a 2022 panel on our democracy. "I mean, we are on the brink of something very new and very challenging. So it is not easy to find solutions, best practices elsewhere; *the creation of a truly multiracial democracy is uncharted territory.*"[89]

That territory—which goes beyond race to include all groups who consider America their home—cannot be charted by our government alone. Sure, the three constitutional branches of our government have the power to pass and rule on laws that could strengthen our democracy and protect the rights of citizens, if they choose. But they can always choose not to, and when political expediency requires it, they have.

> **We cannot afford to delegate the future of our democracy, especially when We the People have the power to do something we are uniquely positioned to do.**

---

[88] By the end of 1965, 250,000 new Black voters were registered. See https://www.aclu.org/voting-rights-act-major-dates-history.

[89] Charles Homans, "Where Does American Democracy Go from Here?" *New York Times Magazine,* March 17, 2022, interview with a panel of six democracy experts. My emphasis.

"No society, no matter how well-equipped it may be technologically, can function without a moral foundation, without convictions that do not depend on convenience, circumstances, or expected advantage," wrote Czech philosopher Jan Patočka. "The point of morality is to assure not the functioning of a society but the humanity of humans."[90]

The humanity of humans.

Who in our society is attending to *that*? Who among us is ensuring that we not lose our humanity, as so many societies riven by strife have done on their way to their deaths? We cannot afford to sink to our lowest nature at the very moment we are called upon by our past dreams and our future challenges to reach for and find the very best in ourselves and in each other.

This is not just a moral task but a practical one. If you and I do not help each other live into the values, ideals, and dreams woven into the hearts and souls of We the People—who will?

That task is our inalienable responsibility as a people.

"I know this sounds really mushy—and I didn't always believe this," said award-winning political scientist Robert Putnam in a May 2023 interview, "but the data and the history have convinced us that the leading indicator [for societal change] is a sense of morality. . . . We need a moral reawakening of America. That's upstream from political choices."

To take moral responsibility for our nation's future is to take responsibility not just for our own well-being but for the well-being of all those groups that make up our democracy. The reason is the same one given long ago by Benjamin Franklin: "We must all hang together or, most assuredly, we shall all hang separately."

Our most formidable enemy today does not lie outside of us. It is not an army or a king like Franklin and his fellow patriots fought. Our most formidable enemy lies inside of us. It is that part in us that looks everywhere but inside and at everyone but ourselves for creating a national reality we do not like.

---

[90] Jan Patočka, "The Obligation to Resist Injustice," in *Jan Patočka: Philosophy and Selected Writings,* ed. Erazim Kohák, (Chicago: University of Chicago Press, 1989), 340–343.

Only we can win the peace with that enemy, and so it is our responsibility to do so. If we succeed, we will safeguard our future as a multigroup democracy. If we fail, we will be failing ourselves. Either way, it is on us.

"The most interesting thing about responsibility," Václav Havel tells us, "is that we carry it with us everywhere. That means that responsibility is ours, that we must accept it and grasp it here, now, in this place in time and space where the Lord has set us down."

EIGHT

WEDDED
to CONFLICT
for BETTER
and for WORSE

History tells us that citizens who shirk their responsibility for preserving democracy do so at their own risk. Just over two millennia ago, citizens in Rome did nothing as democratic norms devolved, obstructionist politics took over, and political violence spilled into the streets, bringing the 482-year-old Roman Republic to an end. In 1930s Germany, Hitler used people's prolonged economic misery to orchestrate an antisemitic, anti-communist campaign that lured citizens into voting him and his Nazis into power, ending the German republic.[91] In 1861, eleven Southern states voted to secede from the United States, throwing our 84-year-old union into civil war. History offers countless warnings: "When citizens look away as their leaders engage in these corrosive behaviors," writes historian Edward J. Watts, "their republic is in mortal danger."[92]

Today one of the biggest risks to our democracy lies not just in our leaders but in our own corrosive behavior as citizens. In Carmel, Indiana, a school board discussion in the winter of 2022 on whether to adopt a curriculum on social-emotional learning and diversity, equity, and inclusion ignited a battle that pitted parents against parents and students against students, with harassed educators caught in the middle on a battleground unlikely to leave anyone standing. One parent took to the podium at the school board meeting, pursed her lips in rage, her voice rising with each word, to warn teachers and board members: "You have lost [the ability] to educate our children. Parents are learning, watching, and

[91] I use the spelling adopted by the Anti-Defamation League: "there is no such thing as a Semitic people."
[92] Edward Watts, *Mortal Republic: How Rome Fell into Tyranny* (New York: Basic Books, 2018).

43

taking action!" Another incensed parent spoke with disdain of those she opposed, "They don't care what we think, they don't care what we say, they don't care how we feel!"[93] No doubt, "they" felt the same way.

Conflict is never going away. For better and for worse, our lives are wedded to conflict, as is our fate. This essay explores how we can make conflict worse or use it to make things better.

When conflicts grow hot, our hot systems kick in

The conflict that erupted in Carmel is an example of what my colleague Amy Edmondson and I call a hot conflict (see Table 8.1). This type of conflict is inherently volatile. This is because the facts of the situation are hard to access, often in dispute, and open to different interpretations; because the situation is risky and the stakes high; because nothing about the present or the future is certain; and because people project onto this screen of uncertainty their different beliefs and interests, leading them to pursue different and often incompatible goals. It is hard to imagine a more reliable recipe for creating the kind of emotional, personal, adversarial discussions that took place at Carmel's school board meeting.[94]

Table 8.1: Hot versus Cool Topics/Conflicts

	Hot Topics/Conflicts	Cool Topics/Conflicts
Data	Hard to access, in dispute, open to different, hard-to-test interpretations	Accessible, verifiable, different interpretations can be tested
Certainty	Relatively low	Relatively high
Stakes	High	Low to moderate
Goals	Informed by different beliefs, interests	Informed by shared beliefs, interests
Discussion	Emotional, personal, adversarial	Reasonable, substantive, collegial

The people battling one another in Carmel are far from alone. Hot conflicts trigger in all of us what psychologists Janet Metcalfe and Walter Mischel call our brain's hot system. Once that system gets activated, we are off and running, reacting reflexively, categorizing people, flattening characters, thinking fast and furious thoughts, leading us to do things we often regret.

[93] See "'They're teaching children to hate America': the culture war in US schools," *Guardian,* February 16, 2022.

[94] See Amy Edmondson and Diana M. Smith, "Too Hot to handle: How to Manage Relationship Conflict," *California Management Review,* vol. 49, no. 1 (Fall 2006). Table 8.1 is adapted from that article.

Table 8.2: Our Brain's Hot and Cool Systems[95]

Hot System	Cool System
Emotional	Thoughtful
"Go now!"	"Know before you go!"
Simplistic	Complex
Reflexive	Reflective
Fast	Slow
Develops early	Develops later in life
Accentuated by stress	Attenuates stress

Their research suggests that this frenzy-making system will continue to hijack our better selves until we do what we all have the potential to do: *help one another slow down and shift back to our cool systems, over and over again, until we can do so more quickly and seamlessly,* freeing us up to generate options that would never occur to any of us while trapped in our hot systems.

The one thing we all agree on is how to disagree

All of us learn from experience some version of the following strategies when hot conflicts break out and our hot systems kick in:

- Fight for our side to win.

- Lobby for our preferred solution, discounting or ignoring adverse effects on others.

- Use point-counterpoint scripts with more or less hostility or civility when debating.

- View our adversarial role as a necessary response to others' adversarial roles.

- See others as more responsible than us for any impasse or stalemate.

- Think of others as mad or bad, ourselves as sane, tame, and not-to-blame.

Not everyone, of course, wants to play by these rules. In "Five Strategies to Support U.S. Democracy," Dr. Rachel Kleinfeld points out that many parents are

[95] Table from Janet Metcalfe and Walter Mischel, "A Hot/Cool-System Analysis of Delay of Gratification: Dynamics of Willpower," *Psychological Review*, 1999. For a similar distinction, see, Daniel Kahneman's book *Thinking, Fast and Slow* makes a similar distinction (New York: Farrar, Straus and Giroux, 2011).

being pushed toward win-lose extremes or silenced. Like many within the quiet majority, these caught-in-the-middle parents hold mixed, complex views. They are more pragmatic. They worry less about divisive cultural issues and more about the impact of prolonged school closures on their kids' education and mental health or about the quality of teaching they saw during Zoom classes.[96] These are common problems that parents can work toward solving together, but too many are stymied by those taking extreme positions and a win-lose, zero-sum approach any time a conflict gets hot.

Some conflicts mask our commonalities and suffocate us all

Journalist and author Amanda Ripley sheds a revealing light on how some conflicts suck us in so deep it is hard to get out.[97] In her bestselling book *High Conflict,* she uses tantalizing tales of conflict, not to lure us in as many journalists might, but to instruct us on how to spot and sidestep malignant conflicts and how to get out should they ensnare us. She draws on one story, study, and statistic after another to catalogue the forces that spark "high conflict"—conflicts that take on a life of their own, suck up all the oxygen in the room, and leave us gasping for air and loaded for bear. She then illustrates how by investigating the "understory" behind such conflicts and by "complicating the narrative," you can uncover "hidden truths" that suggest a way out.

In a 2022 *Washington Post* article, Ripley took this approach to investigating conflicts over school curricula like the one in Carmel, Indiana.[98] Her inquiry into the conflicts' understory showed that groups were filtering what they each said through their own worst fears. Those on the right were worried that those on the left wanted kids to be ashamed of our Founders and our history, while those on the left were worried that those on the right wanted to gloss over slavery and racism. The hidden truth she uncovered was more nuanced. In an interview with More in Common's director of research, Stephen Hawkins, Ripley revealed her findings that neither group believed what the other group feared they did; both

---

[96] Rachel Kleinfeld, "Five Strategies to Support U.S. Democracy," Carnegie Endowment for International Peace, September 15, 2022, https://carnegieendowment.org/2022/09/15/five-strategies-to-support-u.s.-democracy-pub-87918.

[97] Amanda Ripley, *High Conflict: Why We Get Trapped and How We Get Out* (New York: Simon and Schuster, 2021).

[98] Amanda Ripley, "We keep moving from one wrong fight to another. Here's how to stop," *Washington Post*, Opinion, December 8, 2022. Essay 15 in this book also describes what thousands of citizens are doing to ensure we get to know one another again.

groups think we need to address the wrongs of our past while not inhibiting our ability to move forward by making us ashamed of who we are."[99]

So why are we not having *that* conversation? Because of another truth Ripley uncovered in the conflicts' understory: "We are being played by conflict entrepreneurs, people and companies who exploit conflict for their own dysfunctional ends." In this second insight, Ripley sees a way out: "In the months and years to come, we have got to find ways to know one another again. To listen and speak our minds, with dignity and courage."[100]

Putting conflict to work

Just over a hundred years ago, pioneering thinker and social activist Mary Parker Follett proposed a way of seeing conflict that makes it easier for us to listen and speak our minds with dignity and courage. Follett was the first public intellectual to reject zero-sum thinking and to propose that we make conflict do something *for* us. She viewed conflict not as a destructive, "wasteful outbreak of incompatibilities" but as a potentially constructive process through which "valuable differences" can be used to create solutions that benefit everyone. She figured, since conflict is here in the world, since we cannot avoid it, we should set it to work for us. Conflicting groups do not need to coerce one another into doing what they want, nor do they need to settle for unsatisfying compromises. They can work together to invent "mutually satisfying solutions" that no one group alone could imagine. "Coercive power is the curse of the universe," she wrote, "co-active power, the enrichment and advancement of every human soul."[101]

Were Follett privy to the conflict in Carmel, she would point out that everyone in that community likely shares an interest in children being safe and well-educated, even if they hold different views on what that looks like and on how to achieve it. Follett would regard those differences as worthy fodder for problem-solving, as long as they spoke from the heart, listened deeply to one another, checked to see if they understood each other, and focused on their interests, not their positions, in a joint effort to create something new and mutually beneficial.

Like democracy itself, the process would be messy, emotional, and at times frustrating. But hundreds of public policy mediations show how more cooperative

---

[99] See Stephen Hawkins et al., **"Defusing the History Wars:** Finding Common Ground in Teaching America's National Story," More in Common, December 2022, https://rb.gy/luj3mc.

[100] Ripley, "We keep moving."

[101] Mary Parker Follett, *Dynamic Administration: The Collected Papers of Mary Parker Follett*, eds. Elliot M. Fox and Lyndall F. Urwick (Landham, MD: Pittnam, 1973). Almost every book on negotiation and conflict since Follett can be traced back to her writings.

approaches to conflict produce better outcomes. As a graduate student, I studied one such effort in Connecticut where public policy mediators Larry Susskind and Susan Podziba helped a region of twenty-six towns, haggling fruitlessly for ten years, reach a heretofore elusive affordable housing agreement between the fourth poorest city in the U.S. and some of its richest towns. On a global scale, Costa Rican diplomat Christiana Figueres, serving as Executive Secretary of the UN Framework Convention on Climate Change, led a highly inclusive, cooperative negotiation process that produced the 2015 Paris Agreement on Climate Change, unanimously signed by all 197 countries, an exceptional outcome thought unimaginable after the dramatic failure in Copenhagen just six years earlier.

Making the exception the rule

When people see exceptional results like those achieved in Connecticut or in the Paris Agreement, they often discount them, saying they are not replicable. They do not see how others could produce the same results as practitioners as talented as Susskind, Podziba, or Figueres—and thus do not try. Since that could create a self-fulfilling prophecy that stalls human progress, it is worth asking: what does it take to make exceptions the rule?

As a starting point into that question, consider marathoners. At the 1908 London Olympics, U.S. marathoner Johnny Hayes ran the 26.2-mile marathon in just under three hours. It was an exceptional result, the world's best time ever for running a marathon. In 2018 at the Berlin Olympics, another marathoner, Eliud Kipchoge of Kenya, ran the same 26.2 miles in just over *two hours,* cutting Hayes' time by almost a third.

In the intervening years, one generation of marathoners after another had been steadily lowering the curve of time until what was unimaginable in 1908 became doable, even expected, in 2018. Today even ordinary marathoners are running Johnny Hayes' once-exceptional sub-three-hour time, and they are doing it well into their forties *and* without spending anywhere near as much time or effort.

> **The one thing these ordinary runners have in common with their exceptional counterparts is the ability to imagine something better and then push the boundary of what is possible.**

The stories in Parts 2 through 4 shed light on what citizens are doing, largely under the radar and out of our sight, to extend the boundary of what is possible for our multigroup democracy.

PART 2

WALKING

a

NEW ROAD

into

EXISTENCE

Democracy is something that you do. It's something that, when you speak the word, you have to take responsibility for it.

—Timothy Snyder

The future is continually projected from the past onto the screen of the present. What is projected is, in great part, determined by the dreams we hold in common. And for some time now, a large portion of humanity has felt itself to be on a certain enlightened track. It sometimes gets thrown off, but you can still feel the vibration underfoot, with its constant rumbled imperative: Keep laying the rails.

—Patrick Cole

NINE

ON THE EDGE

Blend Images / Alamy Stock Photo

On January 6, 2020, roughly two thousand citizens, some of them armed and all of them inspired by an American president, breached our Capitol in an effort to overturn an election they thought unfair. Whatever you want to call that moment, it threatened 219 years of the peaceful transfer of power. The majority of those involved did not fit the stereotypical violent, extremist profile and had no connection to far-right or White nationalist groups. Most were married, middle-class, middle-aged men with kids and jobs, who belonged to church or community groups, living in pro-Biden or battleground counties. They did not see what they did as anti-democratic but as an act of citizenship.[102] The implication?

---

[102] See Robert A. Pape and Keven Ruby, "The Capitol Rioters Aren't Like Other Extremists," *Atlantic,* February 2, 2021, https://rb.gy/rkkwwi. See also Rachel Kleinfeld, "Five Strategies to Support U.S. Democracy."

Americans who believe in democratic norms should be wary of pat solutions. Some of the standard methods of countering violent extremism—such as promoting employment or waiting patiently for participants to mellow with age— probably won't mollify middle-aged, middle-class insurrectionists. And simply targeting better-established far-right organizations will not prevent people like the Capitol rioters from trying to exercise power by force.[103]

A sobering wake-up call if ever there was one. Yet when Congress launched its inquiry into January 6, most Americans tuned out. Only 28 percent watched some of the hearings, and 57 percent of those were Democrats compared to 32 percent Independents and 25 percent Republicans.[104] Presumably, everyone else was indifferent or viewed the hearings as partisan theater or much ado about nothing. If so, it moved us a little further toward what journalist David Remnick called "a post-truth, post-democratic America," evoking Timothy Snyder's account of Germany's slide into an authoritarian regime: "The hero of a David Lodge novel says that you don't know, when you make love for the last time, that you are making love for the last time. Voting is like that. Some of the Germans who voted for the Nazi Party in 1932 no doubt understood that this might be the last meaningfully free election for some time, but most did not."[105]

Living into the promise of our democracy is an ongoing, centuries-long struggle, a reality many of us find maddening. But abandoning that struggle now will only usher in a single, nonrepresentative minority to determine what is right and just for the rest of us.

In the 1890s, escalating economic and racial inequalities posed even greater threats to our democracy than those today. Politicians were openly bribed; legislation was bought; militias used violence to control workers; communist and anarchist movements were proliferating; and those in power, especially but not exclusively those in the South, sidelined the electorate, harassed political opponents, and relied on state-sponsored violence to impose and enforce racial segregation.[106]

[103] See Pape and Ruby.

[104] William A. Galston, "What are Americans thinking about the January 6 hearings?" Brookings, June 23, 2022, https://rb.gy/ertypx.

[105] David Remnick in the preface to *The January 6th Report* (New York: Celadon Books with *New Yorker*, 2023); Timothy Snyder, *On Tyranny: Twenty Lessons from the Twentieth Century* (New York: Tim Duggan Books, 2017), 28.

[106] Rachel Kleinfeld, "Five Strategies to Support U.S. Democracy."

Yet our democracy survived. In Robert D. Putnam and Shaylyn Romney Grant's book *The Upswing*, the authors recount how enough Americans came together to create a virtuous cycle between civil society and government that shifted the social, economic, and political trends threatening our democracy.

This suggests that if enough of us come together now, we can together write the next chapter of our nation's history as a strong and successful multigroup democracy.

A problem you and I can solve

I doubt any frog dissected in middle school ever underwent the amount of stomach-turning scrutiny given the current state of our nation. Every aspect of its decline has been listed, catalogued, inspected, analyzed, and decried twenty-four hours a day from every political perspective and disciplinary angle possible. Yet very little of this scrutiny sheds light on what you and I can do. In contrast, these essays define a problem you and I can solve.

To recap: The majority of us continue to live within closed, insular, like-minded groups and to distance ourselves from groups different from us, making it easier for us to fear, hate, and compete with one another rather than empathize and cooperate with one another. By not seeing or taking responsibility for our role in this pattern, we contribute to an ungovernable landscape, make ourselves vulnerable to division, and put our democracy and our future at risk.

What you and I can do: By taking the actions summarized in Table 9.1, we can work together across groups on common problems, gradually opening up the closed mental space within groups and closing the distance across them. If, at the same time, we help one another revisit and revise the beliefs that sort and separate us, we can learn to cooperate on building a future in which we make our differences work for us, not against us.

Anyone longing for a better future can take these steps. Whether we choose to do so depends on how well we calculate the costs and benefits of the choice, and on whether we realize how much we have to lose if the space between us again erupts into violence or even civil war.[107]

Too often in our past, we have chosen bullets over ballots. Roughly 620,000 people died during our first and hopefully last civil war, about 2 percent of the

---

[107] See, for example, Ray Dalio, *Principles for Dealing with the Changing World Order: Why Nations Succeed and Fail*; Barbara F. Walter, *How Civil Wars Start: And How to Stop Them*; and Stephen Marche, *The Next Civil War: Dispatches from the American Future*.

Figure 9.1: Action Steps Citizens Can Take

1. **Accept that what brought us to where we are today can take us no further.** Our early survival as a species required us to move from individual collaboration to in-group cooperation, so we could better compete against other groups. Our survival today depends on taking another evolutionary step by cooperating across groups, even those with whom we differ and compete.

2. **Create more space within groups and less across groups.** Clinging to our groups and distancing from other groups divides us and renders us powerless. By opening the insular mental space within groups and closing the distance across them, we can build a future that ensures the survival of all groups without systematically disadvantaging any one group.

3. **Be on the lookout for cultural beliefs, cognitive biases, and emotional defenses that drive us closer to those like us and further away from those different from us.** Our minds all fall prey to cognitive biases and culturally shared beliefs. Our emotional defenses push these biases and beliefs outside our awareness where they are free to run amok, triggering our brain's hot systems. Once triggered, we reduce those in other groups to "flat" characters and turn cross-group conflicts into lose-lose situations. Building a better future depends on our bringing these biases and beliefs into our awareness, so we can revisit and revise those that are harming us, our communities, our democracy, and our futures.

4. **Help one another see what we cannot see, so we can all do better.** Ask those who see us from the *outside-in* to help us see what we cannot see from the *inside-out*: the biases and beliefs evident in those actions that lay outside our awareness. Stop condemning as mad or bad those who deviate from what we think is right, as if we ourselves are always rational and good and right. Instead, help one another within and across groups more fully live into the values we share and learn from those that differ.

population. A war of that magnitude today would take over six million lives, if not far more, given today's weaponry.[108] And while the most polarized among us might be happy to see "the other side" go, it would not resolve our conflicts. It would only launch a new era of violent confrontation between two separate nations.

---

[108] "Statistics From the Civil War," Facing History & Ourselves, last updated August 12, 2022, https://www.facinghistory.org/resource-library/statistics-civil-war.

As disturbing a prospect as that is, it is less likely than an equally disturbing prospect: voters electing an autocrat who cons enough people into thinking that he will end their discontent at the small price of other people's rights and freedoms.[109] All of this is to say:

> **Despite our differences, even those we think irreconcilable, most of us share a profound, even primal self-interest in rejecting that fate and in creating another.**

Social media and twenty-four-hour cable news are not going away, nor are those politicians, corporations, or foreign governments who hope to exploit our differences for their own gain. Unlike these "conflict entrepreneurs," as Amanda Ripley calls them, citizens like you and me share an abiding interest in creating a better future for our nation.[110]

> **It does not take all of us. It takes just enough of us across different groups to inspire a discouraged nation to work together on building a better future.**

In 1835, Alexis de Tocqueville observed a propensity among Americans for coming together and helping one another, especially in times of crisis. That spirit is still very much alive. In July 2023, after torrential rains in Vermont rivaled floods from tropical storm Irene, Vermonters rushed to help one another. "As the water receded Tuesday, the town residents started showing up at the mud-caked, water-scoured store—dozens of them—hauling out damaged goods, emptying freezers, and offering hugs, home-baked cookies, and bottled water."

Within hours, they were organizing mutual aid groups, volunteer groups, and business support systems. "Because we've been through this before," said Vermont's recovery officer after Irene, "we know we need each other and *we know how to work together to do unimaginable and impossible tasks.*" One article said of this working together:

> Resiliency, neighborliness, and community organizing are as much a part of the ethos of Vermont as its maple syrup, ski slopes, and general stores. Each small

---

[109] Robert Kagan, "Our Constitutional Crisis Is Already Here," *Washington Post,* September 9, 2021.

[110] Ripley, *High Conflict.*

town has its own particular interpretation of those characteristics, whether it's showing up to help a flooded store owner in need or adapting to a changing climate.[111]

That ethos—resiliency, neighborliness, community organizing, working together to do unimaginable and impossible tasks—is all deeply embedded in our nation's complicated, imperfect DNA. Every day, you can see that same can-do, come-together spirit at work in communities across our country, peeking through our current discouraged, depressive state to remind us what the news rarely reports: *we are not as helpless or as powerless as we may feel.*

Our times are not so dissimilar to those of 1776. Many people across the colonies then were at least as discouraged as we are now. Deep in the throes of our first American crisis, more and more colonists were losing faith in our fight for independence, just as more and more of us today are losing faith in the future of our democracy. It is easy to see why. The Continental Army was losing one battle after another to the British, just as we are losing one cultural or legislative battle after another to deep-pocketed, anti-democratic forces. The Continental Army was outnumbered, out-trained, out-clothed, out-funded, and underfed. It was hard for people to imagine how those few with so little could possibly overcome the many with so much.

What Thomas Paine said then, he could just as easily say now: "These are times that try men's souls. The summer soldier and the sunshine patriot will, in this crisis, shrink from the service of his country; but he that stands by it now, deserves the love and thanks of man and woman."[112]

Tens of thousands of people in communities across our country are standing by our nation now, activating our instinct to work together to do the unimaginable, impossible tasks it will take to make it through our current crisis.

As the next three essays show, some are taking a stand together against hate and violence; others are using the internet to open up our nation's increasingly insular mental spaces; still others are building coalitions across divides to solve common problems. All of them are turning democracy into a verb on its behalf. Their stories shed a light on how we can make something good out of another time that is trying our souls.

---

[111] Kendra Nordin Beato, Millie Brigaud, "When the floods surged, a focus on readiness helped Vermont," *Christian Science Monitor,* July 14, 2023. My emphasis.

[112] Thomas Paine, *The American Crisis,* 1776.

TEN

TAKING
a STAND

When Mount St. Helens erupted in 1980, it spewed fine volcanic particles into the atmosphere where it formed clouds of ash that wafted down upon Billings, Montana, nine hundred miles east, covering the entire city in an inch of ash. Thirteen years later, Billings felt the effects of a different type of explosion. First, a Native American family returned home to find the word "Dead" and a swastika scrawled on the side of their home. Then self-proclaimed skinheads disrupted a service at an African American church. Then hate flyers were posted near a synagogue, its cemetery desecrated, and a brick thrown through the bedroom window of a six-year-old boy who had placed a menorah there for Hanukkah.

Ian Bassin, who leads Protect Democracy, views events like these as symptomatic of the volcanic times in which we live. As he sees it, forces like globalization, climate change, economic and racial inequities, migration, and tribalism are like shifting tectonic plates under the earth's surface, pushing lava into the base of the volcano, where accelerants like social media, foreign meddling in elections, and partisan polarization are propelling the lava upward. Whereas in the past, democracy's checks and balances could contain the lava's heat and force at the volcano's surface, those same forces that drove lava into the volcano's base have eroded those checks and balances, rendering them too weak to stop the lava from bursting through the top of the volcano. The cumulative result is an explosive rise in divisiveness that, at its most glaring, erupts into violence and at its most insidious, slowly shreds the social fabric holding our multigroup democracy together.[113]

---

[113] Ian Bassin, on a panel at the Virtual Global Democracy Champions Summit sponsored by Keseb, a global nonprofit supporting democracy around the world, and Johns Hopkins University's Agora Institute, strengthening global democracy through powerful civic engagement and informed, inclusive dialogue. Held in May 2022.

In 1993, even Billings, Montana—a vibrant energy center in the Northwest with a predominantly White population and a growing economy—could not escape the effects of societal shifts any more than it could escape the effects of Mount St. Helens' volcanic explosion. The people in Billings learned, as we are all learning, that there is no place to hide in this ever smaller, more connected world of ours. In this world, we will need to create new kinds of checks and balances, ones that go beyond what a democratic government can provide.

We need checks and balances anchored in communities and led by citizens committed to promoting democratic laws, values, and norms whenever and wherever they are threatened.

The citizens of Billings intuitively understood this. That's why, after skinheads targeted an African American church, White neighbors came together to escort churchgoers into the church and attend its services. And that's why, when hateful graffiti appeared on the home of a Native American neighbor, thirty members of the local painters' union came and painted over it. "I was really glad to help paint the house," said one of the painters, "and more so to help convey a message to these guys that the community will not stand for that." And that's why, when a brick shattered a six-year-old's window, hundreds of citizens across Billings put a menorah in each of their windows. "These are our neighbors," union organizer Randy Siemers said of the response. "If someone throws a brick into your neighbor's house, in Montana you run out there and try to stop them. Don't they do that anywhere else in the country?"

Maybe not so much in 1993, but a lot more do now, especially after independent filmmakers Patrice O'Neill and Rhian Miller of the Oakland-based Working Group sent a film crew to Billings to document ordinary people standing up for their neighbors. Curious to see what other communities would make of Billings' response, O'Neill showed the documentary in a small California town. "There were teachers, students, rabbis, priests, and city councilmembers," recounts O'Neill. "When the film ended, they didn't want to talk about Billings. They wanted to talk about their town. They wanted to talk about how people were treated in their community."[114] That got O'Neill thinking. "What if we could do ten town hall meetings around the country, like this one, to see if people could

---

[114] Center for Media and Social Impact (CMSI) interview, https://cmsimpact.org/resource/pull-focus -patrice-oneill/.

open up a conversation, not just about hate crimes but about how we treat each other, how we deal with each other in our everyday lives." Then those ten town hall meetings turned into a hundred, and then a PBS special aired the film *Not In Our Town*.[115] After that, hundreds of screenings took place, and soon those screenings turned into citizen-led groups actively working to build a sense of belonging to reduce hate and violence in their communities.

Twenty-five years ago, O'Neill never would have guessed that a single story could launch a movement.[116] Yet it did. Today hundreds of self-organized Not In Our Town (NIOT) citizen groups are mobilizing faith-based organizations, non-profits, law enforcement agencies, educators, public TV stations, labor organizations, and others to turn bystanders into "upstanders" and to shift community norms away from hate and toward loving thy neighbor.

Figure 10.1: Not In Our Town Citizen Groups

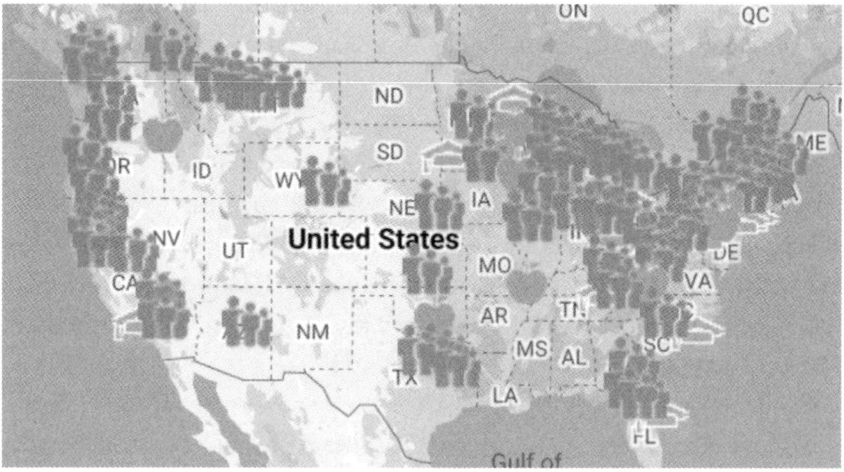

Source: Not In Our Town website

The actions undertaken by the people of Billings, replicated across the country, reveal an often overlooked truth: ***societal shifts are inevitable; our responses to those shifts are not.*** Many communities across our nation are demonstrating the power within our reach when, in response to adversity, we choose to work together on common problems toward a common goal. In making that choice,

[115] To see the PBS special, go to https://www.youtube.com/watch?v=rDH4gKDw_fo.

[116] For more on Not In Our Town (the movement), go to https://www.niot.org/about-us. Also see https://www.niot.org/how-to-start-niot-group.

these citizens are buying us the time we need to reimagine ourselves as a multi-group democracy that encompasses us all.[117]

In his foreword to Jon Alexander's book *Citizens,* musician Brian Eno speaks to this mostly unnoticed movement gaining momentum across the country:

> A different story is rising and ripening. It is a story of who we are as humans, what we are capable of, and how we might work together to reimagine and rebuild our world. This story does not show up on the media radar because that radar is resolutely pointed in the wrong direction. It's expecting the future to be produced by governments and billionaires and celebrities, so its gaze is riveted on them. But behind their backs, the new story is coming together. It is slower, more diffuse, and more chaotic, because it is a story of widely distributed power, not of traditional power centres.[118]

It is easy to underestimate the power of citizens quietly laying the rails toward a better future, but it would be wrong to do so. As anthropologist Margaret Mead is said to have put it: "Never doubt that a small group of thoughtful, committed citizens can change the world. Indeed, it is the only thing that ever has."[119]

---

[117] For another example, also in Montana, see Elizabeth Williamson, "How a Small Town Silenced a Neo-Nazi Hate Campaign," *New York Times*, September 5, 2021, https://www.nytimes.com/2021/09/05/us/politics/nazi-whitefish-charlottesville.html.

[118] Foreword to Jon Alexander and Ariane Conrad's *Citizens: Why the Key to Fixing Everything Is All of Us* (Kingston upon Thames: Canbury Press, 2022).

[119] Nancy C. Lutkehaus, *Margaret Mead: The Making of an American Icon* (Princeton, NJ: Princeton University Press, 2008), 261. Controversy exists over when, where, or even whether Mead ever uttered these exact words, but all agree she held the belief: http://www.interculturalstudies.org/faq.html#quote. And while some quibble with the last sentence, I forgive the hyperbole.

ELEVEN

UNLOCKING OUR MINDS

We all live our lives in groups that afford us more or less mental space, more or less freedom to think independently. The more closed and insular a group, the more likely it is to recirculate the same "facts," retell the same stories, and rehash the same views, its ideology and mythology eclipsing our identities and solidifying our beliefs.

Today more and more groups are growing more and more closed and insular. Even groups who pride themselves on their open-mindedness, their grasp of facts, and their understanding of history and current events are no longer immune. In a world segmented physically and virtually, we cannot help but view the world through the prism of our group's ideas and ideals, filtered and shaped by social and mainstream media on the left and the right. It is the odd one out who ventures to learn what the "other side" is seeing, reading, and hearing. Most of us are not so inclined, and should we accidentally catch a glimpse of the news or books "the other" is consuming, most of us would feel disdain, or ridicule and quickly turn away.

All of us in the United States are grappling with an age-old problem: "How to overcome the blockages to plurality that plurality itself presents us," as author Jon Nixon put it in *Hannah Arendt and the Politics of Friendship.*[120] Perhaps no one has thought more deeply about plurality than Hannah Arendt. After decades of close study, she arrived at a surprising conclusion:

> **The totalitarianism that arose in Nazi Germany and Stalinist Russia was not the problem. It was the most horrific solution to a problem confronting all of humanity: how to live in a pluralist world.**

[120] Jon Nixon, *Hannah Arendt and the Politics of Friendship* (London: Bloomsbury Academic, 2015).

In Arendt's view, the problems caused by plurality are best solved not through one or another type of leader but through the connective tissue of relationships. She grew convinced that the power to resist totalitarianism lay in the space between us, because power can only be activated when we human beings think and act together.[121] Arendt came to this unusual insight after many years spent studying how tyranny takes root and observing the same pattern again and again: "terror can only rule over men who are isolated against each other . . . therefore, one of the primary concerns of all tyrannical government is to bring this isolation about."[122]

Unlocking a nation's closed mental spaces

On an Instagram site visited by over a million people, former high school teacher Sharon McMahon has been inviting citizens to think together about some of our most flammable issues: abortion, immigration, race, and poverty. Since launching the site, McMahon has served as America's government-history teacher at Sharonsaysso: a nonpartisan, factual source of accessible information, explored and discussed in workshops, political sharing sessions, book clubs, and private discussion groups. McMahon estimates that 60 to 70 percent of her now 1 million (and still growing) followers are politically homeless, feel unhappy with the current system, and do not see the America they want to see.[123] That sounds an awful lot like the 87 percent of us that More in Common identified in their Hidden Tribes of America project.[124]

McMahon's secret sauce is her *use of verifiable facts, genuine questions, balanced reasoning, and authentic conversation, offered up in an effort to learn and to help, not convince, cajole, or castigate*. This secret sauce is what allows her to turn toxicity into curiosity and to create a safe space for a wide range of people and views. In that space, McMahon helps people across disparate groups deepen their understanding of one another and the complex, value-laden issues that have divided them, so they can see their common humanity and a common path forward. Writer Elaine Godfrey captures the magic of McMahon's

---

[121] Ibid.

[122] Hannah Arendt, *The Origins of Totalitarianism* (New York: Mariner Books, New Edition, 1976), Kindle Ed., 475.

[123] See Elaine Godfrey, "Sharon McMahon Has No Use for Rage-Baiting," *Atlantic*, June 2022.

[124] See More in Common's 2018 Report *Hidden Tribes of America*.

approach in an *Atlantic* article that opens with an account of a workshop led by McMahon on abortion:[125]

> [The workshop] was not meant to persuade anyone. But by the end of the 2,000-person, five-hour Zoom history lesson, at least a few attendees were thinking differently about one of the most fraught topics in American politics. "I personally believe in the sacredness of life," Shelley Smith, a conservative participant from California, told me afterward. But "something that was important for me to learn was [that] my personal beliefs shouldn't trump someone else's body autonomy."
>
> . . . Hearing information that challenges our beliefs does not usually feel good. Yet participants in McMahon's abortion workshop did not seem to want the lesson to end. They listened as she described early case law and the right to privacy. They peppered her with questions about "personhood" and "viability"; they divulged personal stories, and shared their most closely held religious views. The Zoom chat filled up with reassurances whenever someone raised their hand: *Thank you for bravely speaking up.* One woman asked McMahon whether lawmakers should be allowed to use their religion to justify banning abortion. "That is the million-dollar question, Courtney!" McMahon replied. "All of society's laws are based on a society's morals. Where do people's morals come from?"

Unlike so much of what you find on social media, this virtual, nationwide conversation is anchored in verifiable facts, put in a historical context, explored with curiosity, and pursued without rancor or ridicule. Instead of disdain, those raising controversial questions and views get support for raising good questions and for bravely sharing what they really think and doing so respectfully.[126] Through this collective inquiry, those in the workshop come to realize that ***they need to find out a lot more about the issues about which they feel so strongly. They will need to ask more questions, listen more, and seek out opinions different from their own.***

The one-million-plus subscribers to Sharonsaysso are all engaged in cross-group conversations among friends more interested in learning than in winning points. They are together proving that we can replicate at scale efforts to open our nation's insular mental spaces.

---

[125] See Godfrey, "Sharon McMahon Has No Use for Rage-Baiting."

[126] Compare with Peter T. Coleman and Katharina Kugler's research suggesting that framings that refer to a complex set of challenges related to a focal issue led to more positive emotions and to thinking about the issues in more nuanced, sophisticated ways than more simplistic framing that referred to pro-con, binary choices: Coleman, *The Way Out,* 217.

Giving hate a little competition

McMahon did not set out to have this impact. Like so many of us, she just got fed up. People everywhere were struggling to get the facts, to figure out what was really going on, to grab on to something or someone they could trust. It upset McMahon that so many of them were drowning in a sea of lies and misinformation, much of it hateful.

"I honestly don't think people believe they can get the facts," McMahon told Trevor Noah on *The Daily Show*. "That is really the crux of the matter. They don't understand where to get facts. They don't know who to trust. They feel like they are getting played every day. When they saw I am not a politician, I don't work for some big company, I am literally just a teacher, that has just resonated with some people."

This past year I kept fantasizing about what might happen if someone on the internet gave hate and lies a little competition, if someone created a kind of "Gracebook" to siphon off Facebook's attention-getting power and used that power to feature and fuel acts of grace, kindness, empathy, understanding, and learning. McMahon has done that.

One follower told Godfrey, "I think people are craving goodness. We've created a climate where controversy and hate and contention make money. Sharon created the complete opposite—and it's working."

Instead of igniting a race to the bottom of our brain stems, McMahon's Instagram site is sending us straight to our frontal lobes, where our highest and best thinking resides.

It just goes to show what one thoughtful, committed, fed-up citizen can do. The next essay shows what one coalition of citizens can do.

TWELVE

COMING TOGETHER

The old textile mill town of Lewiston, Maine, was barely scraping by as one millennium gave way to another in the year 2000. Located in the southwest corner of the state, Lewiston is the second-largest city in Maine, bordered on its westernmost edge by the 178-mile Androscoggin River that empties into the Gulf of Maine just 47 miles south. In the mid-1800s, that river attracted a number of investors, including railroad tycoon Benjamin Bates, who turned the growing farm town into a manufacturing center after founding the Bates Manufacturing Company, a five-mill textile center modeled after the one in Lowell, Massachusetts. That industrial center, like others perched along rivers in New England not far from the coast, thrived for over a hundred years before technological and economic changes closed them down or sent them south or abroad for cheaper labor.

In just thirty years, thousands of jobs at Bates disappeared, dropping from 6,751 jobs in 1951 to 950 in the mid-1970s to just 22 in 1990 when, unable to pay its taxes, Bates Manufacturing closed its doors. With the economic heart of Lewiston no longer beating, real estate owners abandoned their buildings, and chain stores left the city for malls on its outskirts. The town was dying, and its people were leaving in droves.

This story of a dying town has touched the lives of hundreds of thousands of people across our nation, leaving them out of work, desperate, angry, and vulnerable to exploitation. If what happened to Lewiston has not happened to you or your town, it is only for the grace of God or the fickleness of economic forces equally hard to fathom.

Imagine what it must be like: your life's work slips away, you can no longer support your family, your kids are hungry and struggling in poor schools, your future is no longer imaginable, or if it is imaginable, you don't want to think about it, and you'll do anything you can—drink, take drugs, toy with suicide— to blot it out. Worse, it all feels beyond your control, totally beyond your control.

Sam T/Flickr from *Only in Your State*, February 19, 2016, Bates Mill #5,
part of a hulking brick textile factory, once the backbone of the Lewiston economy.

There is not one single thing you can do about the global, economic, and technological forces bearing down on your town, your family, your job, and you.

The yearning for certainty and control in the face of uncertain forces outside
your control is unquenchable, and plenty of people seeking to get or keep power
know boatloads about how to exploit it. I imagine that after decades of losing
jobs and losing face, the people of Lewiston felt about as powerless as a people
can feel, primed and ready to defend what little was still "theirs" from "those
people" they feared would replace them.

A surprising turn

It is at this point in the Lewiston story that Heather McGhee picks up the narrative in *The Sum of Us*.[127] By 2000, the jobs and people leaving Lewiston had
created a vicious cycle: "as young people left to find work, there was nobody to
work the few service sector jobs that remained in the wake of shuttered factories.
Then, with the town losing population year after year, it was impossible to attract
new employers." The population that remained in Lewiston was 96.7 percent
White in the whitest and oldest state in the nation and one of only two states
where deaths exceeded births. Into this literal and figurative death spiral entered

---

[127] For the full Lewiston story and its lessons, see Heather McGhee, Chapter 10: "The Solidarity Dividend," in *The Sum of Us: What Racism Costs Everyone and How We Can Prosper Together* (New York: One
World, 2021), Kindle Ed., 246–260.

Lewiston's new deputy city administrator, Phil Nadeau. He was convinced that there was only one way to disrupt this cycle of decline and save the town: more people. "You can't convince businesses to either expand or move into . . . your community if the bodies aren't there," Nadeau told McGhee.

Attracting young, new people to the city and keeping them there, Nadeau realized, would mean attracting refugees entering the United States in search of homes, jobs, and safety, many of them people of color from Africa, Asia, or Latin America. As the happenstance of larger forces would have it, the same year Nadeau took his job in 1999, the U.S. government sponsored a program to resettle thousands of refugees from strife-ridden, famine-stricken Somalia in large cities across the U.S., where formal support systems could ease their transition and integration. After two years in Atlanta, Georgia, one thousand Somalis migrated north to Lewiston, after hearing through the refugee grapevine that crime was low, schools good, and housing cheap.

And this is when the standard tale of a dying town takes a surprising turn. Unlike most communities decimated by decline, Lewiston found a way to rebound.[128] The more Somalis arrived, the better the town's prospects became. As Will Clements of Tufts University's Fletcher School tells it, "With the refugees' arrival, Lewiston became one of the fastest-growing communities in Maine. The crime rate declined, rent prices stabilized, and the city's economy and population have continued to grow ever since."[129] Nadeau told McGhee how previously vacant apartments were now filled, and how long-closed store fronts were now open and full of life. He boasted that while other small towns in Maine had "plummeting real estate values, fleeing young people, and shuttering schools, Lewiston is building new schools—and creating the jobs that come with that."[130] A bipartisan think tank calculated that Maine's African immigrant households contributed $194 million in state and local taxes in 2018. According to McGhee, many "old Mainers" could now see for themselves that these "new Mainers" were not taking anything away from their town; they were contributing to it. As McGhee recounts:

> In many of these communities, longtime residents—who are overwhelmingly
> White—have chosen not to feel threatened by these new people of color. The

[128] Will Clements, "Somali Refugees in Maine: Social Capital in Non-Urban Communities," *The Journeys Project* at Tufts University's Fletcher School, September 1, 2021, https://sites.tufts.edu/journeysproject /somali-refugees-in-maine/#.

[129] Will Clements, "Social Capital and the Success of Refugees in Non-Urban Communities," Henry J. Leir Institute, Tufts University, September 2021.

[130] Heather McGhee, "The Solidarity Dividend," in *The Sum of Us*, 249.

temptation is there, and the encouragement from anti-immigrant politicians is certainly there, but the growth and prosperity the new people bring give the lie to the zero-sum model. Locals know that the alternative to new people is compounding losses: factories, residents, then the hospitals and schools and the attendant jobs. So, the residents are putting aside prejudices in order to grow their home towns, together.

The return of the wedge strategy

The path toward greater cross-group cooperation does not travel in a straight line, however. It is full of loops, mazes, twists, turns, ups, and downs. One day you take an unexpected leap forward, the next a sudden reversal, then three steps forward the week after. Such was the case in Lewiston. A Somali business owner who told McGhee that White and African Mainers got on well, playing sports and doing business together, said he still worried. "The politicians will try to separate us," he said, just as they had in Central and Southern Africa.

His words proved prescient. In 2002, not long after the first Somalis settled in Lewiston, recently elected Mayor Laurier T. Raymond Jr. penned an open letter to the Somali community, saying that the rapid influx of refugees was overwhelming city services, and asking them to slow down the arrival of new refugees. As happened in Carmel, Indiana, different groups with different beliefs saw different things in the letter and reacted differently to it. Some attacked Raymond, calling his letter racially motivated and accusing him of being a racist. Others said he was just doing his job, watching out for the finances of the city. Still others disagreed with the letter but thought his intentions were good.[131] Soon fights broke out, and the ensuing controversy attracted the notice of the *New York Times* and *Washington Post,* whose headlines brought White nationalists to town with their Confederate flags, fabrications about Somali terrorists, and myths about refugees taking things away from White Mainers. Whatever his intentions, Lewiston's mayor had confirmed a Somali business owner's worst fears, driving a wedge between the Black and White, old and new Mainers who, desperate not to lose their footing, fought among themselves.

Eight years later, when Paul LePage ran for governor of Maine in 2010, he made Mayor Raymond look like a unity politician. Every aspect of his campaign presaged the coming of Trump six years later. He said immigrants were stealing

---

[131] Craig Anderson, "Former Lewiston Mayor Laurier T. Raymond Jr. dies at 87," *Portland Press Herald,* May 27, 2019.

resources from local taxpayers when they were in fact contributing millions to the state's coffers; he wanted to lower the minimum wage when those on minimum wage were already unable to support their families; he advocated against welfare for the poor while ensuring it for the rich; he even promoted child labor.

Elected with only 36 percent of the vote in a five-way race, LePage vetoed 652 bills sent to him by the Maine Legislature—more than all governors combined over the previous hundred years. He disparaged every marginalized group in Maine and inflamed debates on every issue that mattered to Mainers. By the time he left office eight years later—having been reelected with 48 percent of the vote in a three-way race—his disapproval rating of 54 percent was the fourth-highest disapproval rating of all governors across the nation.[132] Though never the choice of the majority of Mainers, LePage got elected the old-fashioned way: by playing to a large minority's fears, many of whom, like those in Lewiston, were desperately trying to dig their way out of poverty and despair.

A new story emerges

This time, however, the wedge strategy backfired. This time, enough citizens got together to reject the forces of division and build what McGhee called a "beachhead of solidarity," the Maine People's Alliance, a multiracial, working-class coalition of 32,000 new and old Mainers. In the fall of 2017, this Alliance won a series of victories, among them a successful ballot initiative overriding Governor LePage's Medicaid veto, making Maine the first state in the nation to expand Medicaid. They also helped Maine become the first state in the nation to pass ranked-choice voting by referendum, making it harder for politicians like LePage to get elected by a minority of voters. Later on, they helped get a wave of politicians elected who took on the opioid epidemic and passed a paid-time-off law for Maine workers.

The less obvious result is perhaps the most important long term. Many old and new Mainers told McGhee that they now believed differences could be used to improve their lives. That new belief, McGhee says, did not come from theory or ideology. It came from lived experience. "Each of them had a reason to roll up their sleeves and put in the time to make some part of their community work better, and so doing, they had bettered themselves."[133]

The road these Mainers took to working together was nothing if not uncertain. No one could predict whether their efforts would be worth it, whether

---

[132] See Governor Paul LePage, Wikipedia, https://en.wikipedia.org/wiki/Paul_LePage.

[133] McGhee, "The Solidarity Dividend," *The Sum of Us,* 256.

the progress they made would be enough to overcome the obstacles they faced. But they understood, consciously or unconsciously, what historian Jon Meacham wrote in his account of John Lewis and the struggle for civil rights: the arc of the moral universe *bends* not *swerves* but "the arc won't even bend, without devoted Americans pressing for the swerve."[134]

So that's what these Mainers did: they pressed for the swerve. Together they built cross-group experiences, alliances, friendships, and communities in the face of powerful forces working to divide them. Many of them shifted their ways of seeing and doing things as a result, viewing their differences in a new light. Imagine what might happen if more of us across communities did what these old and new, Black and White Mainers did. Imagine what our multigroup democracy could do if we, too, pressed for the swerve and persevered no matter the odds or the obstacles. If we did that, what now seems impossible would become inevitable.

---

[134] Jon Meacham, *His Truth Is Marching On: John Lewis and the Power of Hope* (New York: Random House, 2020), Kindle Ed., 7. Meacham's emphasis.

THIRTEEN

MAKING
the
IMPOSSIBLE
INEVITABLE

On March 17, 1776, General William Howe, the forty-seven-year-old commander of 6,500 British troops, abruptly evacuated Boston and retreated to Nova Scotia after almost a year garrisoned in the city. Four months earlier, a relatively inexperienced twenty-five-year-old revolutionary, Colonel Henry Knox, first suggested, then undertook what fellow officers claimed was an impossible task: hauling 62 tons of armaments from the captured Fort Ticonderoga in New York—including a massive 5,000-pound cannon nicknamed "Old Sow"—down the Hudson River

The Noble Train of Artillery by Tom Lovell

Valley and across the Berkshire Mountains to the town of Boston, Massachusetts, all in the dead of winter. Using teamsters, boats, and ox- and horse-drawn sledges, Knox and his men crossed nearly 300 miles of snow-covered forests and swamps and the half-frozen Connecticut and Hudson rivers to reach the outskirts of Boston in February 1776.

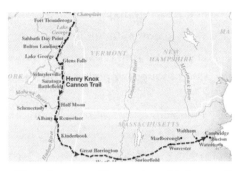

For the previous nine months, the British and American armies had been stuck in a costly stalemate, with neither side strong enough to take the strategic hill of Dorchester Heights needed to dislodge the other. That all changed when Knox accomplished the impossible task of bringing the armaments from Fort Ticonderoga to Boston in midwinter, after which Lieutenant Colonel Rufus Putnam accomplished the impossible task of moving, assembling, and fortifying those armaments onto Dorchester Heights in the middle of the night, while General George Washington accomplished the impossible task of distracting the British with an artillery barrage, so Putnam's painstaking progress up a closely watched hill would go unnoticed.

The next morning, General Washington peered down at Boston Harbor from his perch on the newly fortified Heights while a surprised and dismayed General Howe looked up. Howe's first instinct was to try to retake the hill, but then a snowstorm hit, forcing him to delay. By the time the weather had cleared, Howe reconsidered attacking what was now an American stronghold. Days later, the British general set sail for Nova Scotia with all 120 British ships, inspiring Washington and his Continental Army to persevere, eventually proving victorious.

Disrupting trends

Today we take our independence for granted. We think of it as the inevitable outcome of a war fought by exceptional men. Most colonists at the time saw things differently. They looked at their current trend—one battle lost after another—and could not see a way to their independence.

"Time and again, we mistakenly make straight-line projections about markets or demographics or politics," says democracy expert Lee Drutman, "assuming that whatever trends have led us to this moment, they will continue indefinitely. But they never do."[135]

Twenty-five-year-old Henry Knox was determined to end the Continental Army's losing streak by achieving the impossible. He persisted because he believed what James Baldwin believed: "we can do with this country something that has not been done before . . . It doesn't take numbers; it takes passion."

[135] Lee Drutman, "How Democracies Revive," Niskanen Center, April 2022.

> **In the soil of that passion, a vision for a better future can be sown, and the commitment and determination to realize that vision can take root. From those roots, perseverance will grow until something thought impossible becomes inevitable.**

Thousands of citizens from California to Montana to Maine, on the ground and across the internet, are walking a new road into existence, so we can do with this country something that has not been done before: use the differences that both challenge and enrich us to build a better future for all of us. The stories in Parts 3 and 4 show how citizens are together building that future, each in their own way.

PART 3

REMAKING OUR DEMOCRACY

in

A NEW IMAGE

A friend may be waiting behind a stranger's face.

—Maya Angelou

I don't like that man. I must get to know him better.

—Abraham Lincoln

FOURTEEN

TAKING ANOTHER EVOLUTIONARY STEP

Most of us make friends in separate spaces. As children, we grow up in largely segregated neighborhoods and schools. When we leave home, we form "urban tribes," those largely homogenous, improvised families we create for emotional support as we move out into the world. Then, as busy adults, we narrow our social networks still further.[136]

This "huddling together with the same few people" worries psychologist Dr. Meg Jay.[137] In *Defining Decade,* Jay advises those in their twenties to look outside their like-minded, same-sorted social groups. She might just as well have been talking to all of us. Drawing on Mark Granovetter's work on strong versus weak ties, Jay argues that it is our weak ties, not our strong ties, that have the most to teach us. "It is the people we hardly know—those who never make it into our tribe—who will swiftly and dramatically change our lives for the better." Those with whom we have no ties or only weak ties know things and people we don't; they can give us new perspectives and ideas. Yet, as Jay points out, those with whom we have weak ties "feel too different from us—or literally too far away from us—to be close friends."

[136] See Emily Richmond, "Schools Are More Segregated Today Than During the Late 1960s," *Atlantic,* June 11, 2012; "Segregation in America: 'Dragging On and On,'" NPR's *Morning Edition,* February 18, 2011; and Ethan Watters, *Urban Tribes: A Generation Redefines Friendship, Family, and Commitment* (London: Bloomsbury, 2003).

[137] Meg Jay, *The Defining Decade: Why Your Twenties Matter and How to Make the Most of Them* (New York: Twelve, 2012), 20–22, 32.

There it is again. That space between us: so close within, so distant across. We are just "too far away" to be close friends with those different from us. Sociologists have long studied this tendency of ours to seek out people like us. They call it homophily, love of the same.[138]

> "From the schoolyard to the boardroom," says Dr. Jay, "people are more likely to form close relationships with those most like themselves."

In the 1970s, sociologist Dr. Peter Blau saw more at play here than just a personal choice to flock with those of the same feather. Using large-scale statistical data, Blau was able to reveal the "opportunity structure" underlying our society. That structure separates people into demographically distinct groups that are more or less close to one another, expanding or constraining our opportunities to interact across groups and move up in the world socially, ultimately governing how close or how far we get to that boardroom Dr. Jay mentions.[139]

Not all is lost, however, to a structure seemingly outside our control. In Blau's last book, he proposes that while this structure governs our interactions across groups, those interactions also affect this larger structure. To sociologist Dr. Heather Haveman, this suggests a dynamic system in which the two influence each other.[140] The practical implication for you and me?

> Our interactions across groups have the power to reshape this larger structure and the opportunities and constraints it allocates across groups as a result.

Which scenario will we choose?

In a 2009 *Atlantic* article, writer Hua Hsu reflects on the demographic shifts transforming the face of America from White to multiracial. As he looks out forty years into the future, he imagines two scenarios. In the first, he sees "white

---

[138] My thanks to sociologist and organizational behaviorist Dr. Sameer Srivastava for pointing me to this distinction.

[139] Peter M. Blau, *Structural Contexts of Opportunities* (Chicago: University of Chicago Press, 1994), 4–6, 9–11.

[140] Heather A. Haveman, "Book Review *Structural Contexts of Opportunities* by Peter M. Blau," *American Journal of Sociology*, July 1995. Also, see Heather A. Haveman, *The Power of Organizations: A New Approach to Organizational Theory* (Princeton, NJ: Princeton University Press, 2022).

identity politics growing more potent and more forthright in its racial identifica-
tions . . . as 'the real America' becomes an ever-smaller portion of, well, the real
America, and as the soon-to-be white minority's sense of being besieged and dis-
dained by a multicultural majority grows apace." In the second, he predicts that
while there will be dislocations and resentments along the way, "the demographic
shifts of the next 40 years are likely to reduce the power of racial hierarchies over
everyone's lives, producing a culture that's more likely than any before to treat its
inhabitants as individuals, rather than members of a caste or identity group."[141]

A lot of people have given a lot of thought to how we can avoid the first
scenario and create the second, political theorist Dr. Danielle Allen among them.
She starts with a fundamental fact of democratic life: all citizens in a democracy
must grapple with loss and disappointment when political decisions fail to meet
their interests. Historically, we have dealt with this fact of life, says Allen, by
developing entrenched patterns of domination and acquiescence that apportion
losses disproportionally across groups. If these cross-group patterns persist into
the future, it is hard to see how we can realize Hsu's second scenario. As Frederick
Douglass warned long ago, "Where any one class is made to feel that society is in
an organized conspiracy to oppress, rob, and degrade them, neither persons nor
property will be safe."

To complicate matters, our political system both reinforces and is reinforced
by these cross-group patterns of domination and acquiescence. Long before today's
political dysfunction pushed its way into our daily consciousnesses, award-winning political scientist Dr. Jane Mansbridge anticipated the trouble in *Beyond
Adversary Democracy*. Her close study of two very different communities led her
to conclude that an adversarial conception of democracy, untempered by a more
consensus-oriented model, runs the risk of elevating conflicting interests above all
else, including our shared interests and our common goals as citizens. In *Breaking
the Two-Party Doom Loop*, Lee Drutman describes how our two-party, winner-
takes-all political system has steadily made our democracy more toxic since Mansbridge's early caution, trapping us in either-or, win-lose warfare. The alternative,
Drutman suggests, is to move toward a multiparty system, in which political differences are less binary and more complex, reducing polarization among groups.
In *Citizenship in Hard Times* political scientist Sara Goodman comes to the same
conclusion based on a study of civic obligations in the U.S., Britain, and Germany. She found that two-party, majoritarian systems magnify differences among

---

[141] Hsu, "The End of White America?"

citizens, provide fewer opportunities for consensus, and lead people to view potential gains and losses through a "sharper set of partisan trade-offs."[142]

But here is where the chicken meets the egg. Mounting evidence suggests that political reforms such as fusion voting and proportional representation would help disrupt our current democratic doom loop. But it is awfully hard to garner support for such reforms in a nation with a two-party system caught in a doom loop. Breaking that chicken-and-egg impasse will likely take organized efforts like those undertaken in Maine, where citizens worked together across groups to pass ranked-choice voting.[143]

What will it take for us to work together toward a common goal?

Avoiding Hsu's first scenario and realizing his second will largely depend on the ability of citizens to work creatively and constructively across groups, even when they disagree or suffer the occasional loss or disappointment. To build that ability, we need an alternative to the adversarial model of democracy underlying our current winner-takes-all, win-at-all-costs political system. That model will always lead us to see and treat those different from us as potential adversaries or even enemies, making our increasingly interdependent world increasingly dangerous.

What if, instead of seeing those in different groups as potential adversaries or enemies, we saw them as potential friends? As unimaginable as that might strike you, Danielle Allen imagines for us what might happen:

> Friends know that if we always act according to our interests in an unrestrained fashion, our friendships will not last very long. Friendship teaches us when and where to moderate our interests *for our own sake*. In short, friendship solves the problem of rivalrous self-interest by converting it into equitable self-interest . . . Whereas rivalrous self-interest is a commitment to one's own interests without regard to how they affect others, *equitable self-interest treats the good of others as part of one's own interests*.[144]

---

[142] Jane J. Mansbridge, *Beyond Adversary Democracy* (New York: Basic Books, 1980); Lee Drutman, *Breaking the Two-Party Doom Loop: The Case for a Multiparty Democracy in America* (Oxford, UK: Oxford University Press, 2019); Sara Wallace Goodman, *Citizenship in Hard Times: How Ordinary People Respond to Democratic Threat* (Cambridge, UK: Cambridge University Press, 2022).

[143] For more on Maine, see Essay 12: "Coming Together." For more on electoral reform, see Lee Drutman, "More Parties, Better Parties: The Case for Pro-Parties Democracy Reform" a report from New America. https://rb.gy/bwqtx Although Drutman still thinks RCV is useful in primaries, his review of recent evidence leads him to think that other reforms like proportional representation and fusion voting are more promising.

[144] Allen, *Talking to Strangers*, 126. My emphasis.

Friendship is the great equalizer. It turns flat characters into round ones, so we can see and treat one another more like the individuals we are, rather than simply members of a caste or identity group. Friendship helps us work through our conflicts, differences, and disappointments, because we care about what happens to our friends, not just us. We rely on our friends, and they rely on us, building the mutual trust that allows friendships to last in the face of hard times.

As a model for democratic citizenship, friendships that cross boundaries have an unparalleled competitive advantage. Instead of creating patterns of domination and acquiescence in the face of loss and conflict, they would create patterns of reciprocity and mutuality, especially when it comes to our rights and responsibilities in relation to one another. We would understand that even if we have the right to do something, it may not be the right or responsible thing to do with a friend upon whom we depend to do the right and responsible thing with us. Instead of exhausting the trust and goodwill needed to make our pluralist endeavor a success, cross-group friendships would revive both. Seeing ourselves as friends, we would act like friends, making sure no one group bears the brunt of society's losses over time. In short:

> **As friends, we can build a future far better and safer than any we can build within our adversarial model of democracy and the patterns of dominance and acquiescence it sustains.**

The person who puts it best is the one who has thought longest about the limits to our adversarial form of democracy. "Our [form of democracy] cannot handle the highly complex interdependence of today's world," Jane Mansbridge said in a recent email. "Party systems that structurally pit party against party and politician against politician as enemies undercut a nation's capacities for building commonality and negotiating conflict."[145]

The practical, political relevance of friendship

Isolation is a breeding ground for fear and hate. In 2013, sixteen-year-old Mak Kapetanovic found himself alone after his mother died of a stroke.[146] With his father working nights and no siblings at home, Mak sought company online,

---

[145] From a recent email sent to me and Bruce Patton.

[146] This account is based on Charlotte McDonald-Gibson, "How Coronavirus Creates the Perfect Breeding Ground for Online Extremism," *Time*, March 26, 2020.

spending up to six hours a day on far-right talkboards where he was bombarded with "a flood of racist rhetoric."

Mak was not a typical target of ultra-right extremist groups. He was the child of Bosnian Muslim refugees. Even so, within months, he found himself believing the antisemitic, racist messages in which he had immersed himself to ward off feelings of isolation and loneliness. Unlike most of those taking Mak's path, he decided to look into far-right claims about race and intelligence, and finding no reliable sources, he gradually disavowed the ideology.

He now uses his experience to educate people who are looking for virtual love in all the wrong places. He explains how far-right groups recruit followers online by exploiting their loneliness. In retrospect, he wishes more people had reached out to him, and he advises us to reach out to others: "Check up on your friends and make sure everyone is doing OK."

In May 2023, Surgeon General Vivek Murthy issued a public health advisory warning that loneliness and isolation have reached epidemic proportions.[147] Three months later, in "The Weaponization of Loneliness," Hillary Rodham Clinton cited the Surgeon General's study along with Robert Putnam's seminal book *Bowling Alone* to draw attention to how this epidemic is no longer just harming our mental and physical health but also weakening our democracy's immune system—those social and community structures that tether us to one another. Clinton recounts how ultra-right political operative Steve Bannon exploited the resulting fragmentation:

> [Bannon] discovered an army of what he later described as "rootless white males," disconnected from the real world but highly engaged online . . . When Bannon took over the hard-right website *Breitbart News*, he was determined to turn these socially isolated gamers into the shock troops of the alt-right, . . . [As] a senior executive at Cambridge Analytica, . . . Bannon targeted "incels," or involuntarily celibate men, because they were easy to manipulate and prone to believing conspiracy theories. "You can activate that army," Bannon told the *Bloomberg* journalist Joshua Green. "They come in through Gamergate or whatever and then get turned onto politics and Trump."[148]

Clinton goes on to sum up the result, not just of isolation and loneliness but of those preying on the isolated and lonely for their own divisive ends:

---

[147] Vivek Murthy, "Our Epidemic of Loneliness and Isolation: The U.S. Surgeon General's Advisory on the Healing Effects of Social Connection and Community," May 2023.

[148] Hillary Rodham Clinton, "The Weaponization of Loneliness," *Atlantic*, August 7, 2023.

"intensifying political polarization, economic inequality, loss of trust in government, and a shift in the national attitude from 'we're all in this together' to 'you're on your own.'"[149]

"It's unhappiness, stupid!"

In a 2023 *Democracy* article, behavioral scientist George Ward describes how mounting isolation and loneliness is fueling a disturbing decrease in happiness. In 2021, only 19 percent of Americans surveyed said they felt happy, the lowest level since 1972. The resulting increase in unhappiness is not only leading to more "deaths of despair," it is also shaping voting behavior. Says Wards' colleague Johannes Eichstaedt: [150]

> "Unhappiness predicted the Trump vote better than race, income levels, or unemployment, how many immigrants moved into the country, or how older or religious citizens were. Unhappiness also predicted the Trump election better than other subjective variables like how people *thought* the economy was going or would be going in the future.

If isolation and loneliness is the unhappy epidemic fracturing our society, then friendship is the cure. Ten years after the Holocaust, Hannah Arendt made a case for the political importance of friendship. "We are wont to see friendship solely as a phenomenon of intimacy, in which the friends open their hearts to each other unmolested by the world and its demands," she wrote. "Thus it is hard for us to understand the political relevance of friendship." Its relevance for Arendt lay in the power of cross-group friendships to resist authoritarian efforts to first isolate and then pit groups against one another.

Resisting authoritarian efforts today is at least as hard as it was in Arendt's time. The space between us has turned us into a nation of strangers and, at times, enemies. Some evangelical Christians are going so far as to reject Jesus's teachings to love thine enemy and turn the other cheek, telling their pastors, "That doesn't work anymore. That's weak."[151]

[149] Ibid.

[150] Deepak Bhargava, Shahrzad Shams, and Harry Hanbury, "The Death of Deliverism" in *Democracy*, June 2023 at https://rb.gy/8dqdp. Also see George Ward, "It's Unhappiness, Stupid." The Society for Personality and Social Psychology, June 2021. https://rb.gy/ieybe.

[151] Tori Otten, "*Christianity Today* Editor: Evangelicals Call Jesus 'Liberal' and 'Weak,'" *New Republic*, August 10, 2023.

> **How can we possibly cross the distance between us to become friends in such a world?**

Arendt gives us a few pointers. She describes how, through conversations over time, strangers from vastly different worlds become friends, as they talk about the same things. Through these conversations, friends who were once strangers create a shared world of their own.[152] In this now-shared world, they do not so much bridge their differences as integrate them into a new understanding of one another, themselves, and the world around them. As the stories in the next three essays bring to life, those conversations and that understanding help newfound friends take the best from each other and use it to build a better future together.

The role of cross-group friendships

When circumstances many millennia ago grew more complex than our early ancestors could handle, they adapted accordingly. They took two evolutionary steps toward greater cooperation.[153] In the first step, recounts anthropologists Dr. Michael Tomasello and his colleagues, they moved from foraging as individuals to collaborative foraging to ensure greater safety and success at hunting stags, a step that cultivated an interest in the well-being of their foraging partners. When they then faced even greater complexity and competition, they took a second step. Building on the first step's collaborative motivation and skills, they established group-level cooperation based on group-minded structures and norms that, among other things, demarcated each of us as members of one or another group.

Skip a few millennia to the Age of Enlightenment, and we find a group of educated, well-off Europeans advancing a set of beliefs to explain, justify, and maintain a social order built on this evolutionary heritage: some groups are innately superior to others, one group's gain necessarily comes at another's loss, and it is an inherently win-lose world. Those vestigial beliefs are now making it harder for us to take a third evolutionary step needed to survive today—namely, moving from in-group cooperation to cross-group cooperation in much the same way early humans moved from individual collaboration to in-group cooperation.

---

[152] From Hannah Arendt, "Philosophy and Politics," cited in Aaron Schutz and Marie Sandy, "Friendship and the Public Stage: Revisiting Hannah Arendt's Resistance to 'Political Education,'" *Educational Theory*, vol. 61, no. 1 (February 2015).

[153] Tomasello et al., "Two Key Steps."

> You would think if our early ancestors could take an evolutionary step to ensure their survival, we could take one to ensure ours. After all, they were quite literally Neanderthals.[154]

Some within the business community are already moving in this direction to adapt to an environment in which competitors in one realm or at one time need to cooperate in another. To manage that complexity, business leaders invented a practice called "coopetition," in which businesses no longer treat competitors as adversaries or enemies but as respected colleagues with whom they both cooperate and compete. This new practice has allowed them to sustain cross-group relationships under highly complex, constantly changing circumstances.

But exactly how do you take this new evolutionary step as a species? Recent research in social psychology suggests a way to put this new step under our everyday control: build cross-group friendships. According to this research, cross-group friendships are the ideal kind of intergroup contact to improve cross-group cooperation, and it takes just one cross-group friend to increase our receptivity to further cross-group interactions and to initiate more interactions in the future.[155] The implication? The more of us who build cross-group friendships, the more successfully we can adapt to today's more complex, interdependent world.

That is why the next three essays focus on cross-group friendships. Each essay tells a story about improbable friendships made across some of our starkest lines of difference in three tumultuous contexts: polarized political parties in Congress before and after January 6; religions and race in a highly segregated city after an antisemitic terrorist attack; and clashing ideologies on the far right and left in a liberal arts college.

These stories of friendship built across divides in unfriendly contexts demonstrate what is possible under conditions many of us may never face. Their hard-earned lessons give us much-needed guidance on how to move up the continuum of difference in our own hopefully less adverse circumstances. The further we move up that continuum, the more we will open the mental space within our own groups and close the distance across groups, allowing us to cooperate with one another on building a better future.

---

[154] For those wondering, this is a joke, not a scholarly assertion about the role Neanderthals played in taking that second step. The point, however, remains: we can evolve in much the same way our ancestors did.

[155] Elizabeth Page-Gould, Rodolfo Mendoza-Denton, and Linda R. Tropp, "With a Little Help from My Cross-Group Friend: Reducing Anxiety in Intergroup Contexts through Cross-Group Friendship," *Journal of Personality and Social Psychology*, vol. 95, no. 5 (2008); Elizabeth Page-Gould, Kelci Harris, Cara C. MacInnis, Chad M. Danyluck, and Ian D. Miller, "The Intergroup Perspective on Cross-Group Friendship," *Advances in Experimental Social Psychology*, vol. 65 (2022): 1–56.

FIFTEEN

RENOVATING
the
PEOPLE'S
HOUSE

"I ran for Congress to make a difference. Now that I'm here, I might as well be a potted plant." That is how one Congressional Representative summed up his and many of his colleagues' experience in one of sixty interviews conducted in 2018 by conflict expert Bruce Patton and his colleagues at the Rebuild Congress Initiative (RCI).[156]

Although January 6 was still two years away, plenty else had already happened to erode trust, drive parties apart, and make it harder to get things done in the "People's House": demographic shifts in and outside of Congress, economic dislocations in Congressional districts, the explosion of twenty-four-hour cable news and AI-driven social media, the unrestrained injection of money into politics, the election of our first Black president followed by a racially divisive one.

The list goes on, driving greater ideological cohesion within parties and greater distance between them. As you might expect, this growing closer within and more distant across drove members of Congress toward more extreme positions, making collaboration and progress more difficult, just as it has for citizens across the country. Over the past fifty years, this has led both parties in Congress to migrate

---

[156] For more on RCI, go to https://www.rebuildcongress.org. Full disclosure: Bruce Patton is my husband; those working on this project at RCI are my friends and colleagues; and I have served as an advisor to the RCI team since its inception.

away from the center, though as Table 15.1 illustrates, Republicans have moved significantly further to the right than Democrats have to the left.[157]

Table 15.1: Republicans Have Moved Further to the Right than Democrats Have to the Left

Average ideology of members, by Congress

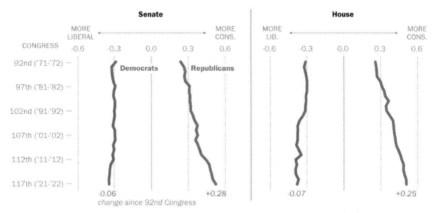

Note: Data excludes nonvoting delegates, as well as lawmakers who officially served but (due to illness, resignation or other factors) didn't have a scorable voting record for a given Congress. Party categories include independents who caucus(ed) with that party. Members who changed parties (or became independents) during a Congress were classified according to the status they held the longest during that Congress. For most of the 116th Congress, Rep. Justin Amash of Michigan was either an independent or a Libertarian, and didn't caucus with either major party.
Source: Pew Research Center analysis of Voteview DW-NOMINATE data accessed on Feb. 18, 2022.

Long-time Republican operative Sarah Longwell, publisher of the *Bulwark*, credits the "Republican triangle of doom" with pushing the Republican Party so far to the right:

> It is the toxic, symbiotic relationship between voters, elected officials, and the right-wing infotainment media working together to push the party further right.
>
> Take something like January 6th or the idea the election was stolen. At first, a portion of the Republican party said, "No, the election wasn't stolen. It was free and fair, and January 6th was a terrible event."
>
> Then over time, the triangle of doom works on itself. The right-wing media says, "No, it was Patriots storming the US Capitol, and the election did look like it was stolen." That then moves more voters to believe the election was stolen.
>
> Voters then put pressure on elected officials, and elected officials come out and say, "January 6th was really just a protest, not an insurrection." And that confirms it for another group of voters.

---

[157] Drew DeSilver, "The polarization in today's Congress has roots that go back decades," Pew Research Center, March 10, 2022.

Before you know it, you've got 70 percent of Republicans believing the 2020 election was stolen, and they're all reinforcing one another.

It's not just one thing.[158]

When RCI conducted their interviews in 2018, Democrats and Republicans were already further apart than at any other time in the past fifty years. That made the House one of the last places you would expect to make friends across party lines. Yet that is where some very important friendships got made in an ambitious, yet largely unheralded, bipartisan effort to reform the way Congress operates.

Early in 2019, by a vote of 418 to 12, the House approved a member-led proposal to create the House Select Committee on the Modernization of Congress with the goal of making the House work better for the American people. That committee, composed of six Democrats and six Republicans, required a two-thirds majority to pass recommendations. In only four years, they nevertheless managed to pass more than 200 recommendations, most unanimously, two-thirds of which are already fully or partly implemented. Spanning two sessions of Congress, one before and one after the January 6 attack on the Capitol, the committee's life was extended twice, and in 2023, it was made a permanent subcommittee of the Committee on House Administration.

Looking back on the committee's work, its chair for both sessions, Representative Derek Kilmer, a Democrat from Washington state, recalls thinking early on, "If you want things to work differently in Congress, then you have to do things differently in Congress."

Doing things differently

That is what Kilmer and his vice-chairs decided to do. Over the lifespan of the committee, Chair Kilmer worked alongside two Republican Vice-Chairs: Representative Thomas Graves of Georgia in the first session and, after Graves' retirement from Congress, Representative William Timmons from South Carolina in the second.

Timmons took on his role as vice chair believing the objective of Congress was to engage in evidence-based policymaking in a collaborative manner from a position of mutual respect. "We don't normally do that," Timmons said. "The

[158] From Christiane Amanpour's interview with Sarah Longwell, "Explaining 'the Republican triangle of doom,'" CNN, April 19, 2022. Edited for brevity and clarity. For the full interview, go to https://rb.gy/gjghc.

biggest challenge is trust. Trust is something that requires a relationship; it requires time getting to know one another. It requires being open to discussing your ideas, to having your ideas challenged by someone you consider a friend, or at least someone who is not going to attack you for a difference of opinion."[159]

Just as Kilmer and Graves became friends and allies in the committee's first session, so did Timmons and Kilmer, building enough trust to disagree and work through those disagreements in the service of a common objective: making progress on behalf of the American people.

"I have a district that actually needs Congress to work," Kilmer said in a 2023 interview. "So I have very little patience for the amount of time and mental energy put towards the battle. I actually think we could get a lot done if we approached each other from a position of mutual respect and tried to solve problems with each other."

The committee's accomplishments provide proof of that concept. Among the decisions on how to operate as a committee, a small number made a big difference, according to Kilmer, Graves, and Timmons. First among them was the decision to schedule a planning retreat before launching the committee's work. "I've never been part of a functional organization that didn't define what success looks like," said Kilmer, "and then figured out a plan for getting there." To ensure success, Kilmer asked Bruce Patton and the Congressional Management Foundation to facilitate by helping members list and diagnose different sources of dysfunction, then set an agenda for addressing them.

Once they had a shared objective and plan, they blew up the standard way of operating as a committee. They decided to make rolling recommendations every quarter rather than waiting for their final report. This motivated them to get more things done and allowed them to track and push implementation. They also discarded the usual staff hiring practice, in which Democrats hire Democrats to wear blue jerseys and Republicans hire Republicans to wear red jerseys. Instead, they hired one staff, made up of Democrats and Republicans, all of whom put on jerseys that said, "Let's fix Congress."

This same-team orientation also led them to redesign the physical space in which they held meetings and hearings. Walk into almost any committee meeting,

---

[159] The interview data in this essay come from two sources: an interview conducted by Bruce Patton of RCI with Reps. Kilmer and Timmons after their committee received an award for their innovative work in Congress from the American Bar Association's section on Dispute Resolution, and an interview conducted by Amanda Ripley for the article, "These radically simple changes helped lawmakers actually get things done," *Washington Post,* February 9, 2023.

and you will see a long dais with Republicans lined up on one side with Democrats facing off against them on the other side. Because they wanted to open up discussions across parties and bring members closer together, they placed Democrats next to Republicans, side by side, usually around a round table. "We wanted people to make eye contact and to have a conversation," Kilmer explained. The change was immediately apparent to the staff in the room. "They were tittering among themselves with texts flying around the Capitol," Patton recalls. "They'd never seen anything like it."

Nor had anyone seen anything like the way they managed time. As a rule, committees are highly structured and tightly scheduled, with each witness and member getting five minutes to give remarks, after which another member gets five minutes, and so on. Because Kilmer, Graves, and Timmons wanted to create the kind of back-and-forth that sparks new insights and ideas, they decided to relax the constraints on time, encouraging in-depth discussions among both members and witnesses. When *High Conflict* author Amanda Ripley testified in front of the committee, the change was almost unnerving. "I'd covered a lot of hearings as a reporter, and they always felt choreographed, stilted and performative. This experience was different. It felt, at times, like members were sharing their genuine fears and asking real questions. It was not obvious who was on which political side, which was at once both disorienting and wonderful."

Few things close the space between groups more than breaking bread together. Perhaps that is why Vice-chair Timmons insisted the committee meet for dinner every few months. Only thing was, "It was absolutely, insanely hard to find the space," he told Ripley. As often happens in polarized environments, the person in charge—in this case, the Speaker of the House—controls almost everything, making it close to impossible to reserve a room for a bipartisan dinner. But Timmons insisted and persisted, and he got it done.

To Timmons, breaking bread, seating people next to each other, and relaxing time constraints were not just cosmetic exercises. "They changed the way things worked. They set us up for success. We sat differently, we interacted differently, we actually spent time together." Kilmer also thinks this is what made the difference. "There's a reason we passed more than 200 bipartisan recommendations; it's because we did things differently." According to Ripley, those results speak for themselves: "The last select committee created to reform Congress, which focused on budgeting, passed exactly zero recommendations by the time it ended in 2018."

No potted plants here. By reshaping the physical, social, even temporal space that constrains interactions between the two parties, the modernization committee built relationships with enough trust to make collaboration and evidence-based policymaking possible.

Digging deeper

When committee members returned to work after January 6, that trust was shattered. Derek Kilmer recounted to Amanda Ripley what it was like to come back to the House after the events of that day.[160]

> He met with all the committee members, one by one, to ask what they wanted to work on. The answer was, basically: *Nothing.* Most didn't think Democrats and Republicans would be able to sit in the same room together, let alone work with each other.
>
> "Some of the conversations were really alarming," Kilmer remembers. One Democrat told him: "I feel like not only was I in a relationship with someone who cheated on me; I was in a relationship with someone who cheated on me *with someone who was trying to kill me . . .*"
>
> "We're screwed," he told his chief of staff. "We're going to have to do some stuff differently."

Figuring out how to do things differently before January 6 was hard enough. But as a management consultant in his prior life, Kilmer knew a lot about how to structure and lead teams. This was totally uncharted territory. To navigate it, Kilmer invited his new Vice Chair, William Timmons, out for "cheap Thai food and expensive Tequila." As they talked, they realized that they would have to dig deeper and take even bigger risks. They would have to start their upcoming planning retreat for this second two-year session with a facilitated conversation, in which each member of the committee would share what they went through on January 6 and how it was affecting their ability to work together. On March 20, 2021, mediator David Fairman from the Consensus Building Institute joined Bruce Patton of RCI to facilitate a conversation with committee members on Zoom due to the pandemic. Kilmer and Timmons broke the ice:

> Kilmer talked about getting texts from the Capitol Police on Jan. 6, telling him to shelter in place. Alone in his office in the Rayburn House Office Building, he

---

[160] This account of how the committee handled January 6 is based on Ripley, 2023, including the quotes.

turned off the lights and pushed the furniture against the door. . . . For about five hours, he watched CNN on mute and texted with his family and his staff. He felt more heartsick than frightened. He thought about how, before he'd left for work, he'd told his kids not to worry about him; after all, he'd told them, he worked in some of the safest buildings in the United States.

Timmons then talked about his own experience that day. He explained that he wanted the protesters who had breached the Capitol to be arrested and held accountable under the law. He wished that President Donald Trump had done more, sooner, to stop them. And, at the same time, he said, he had serious concerns regarding the constitutionality of election-law changes that had been made very quickly in certain states, which was why he'd voted not to certify the election results that night. To Timmons, those things could all be true.

Other members then talked about their experiences, revealing things that not only surprised one another but Fairman as well. "The conversations were quite remarkable," Fairman told Ripley. "They surpassed my expectations."

The now-established committee norm of doing things differently was paying off in a new way. Instead of playing performative roles, members decided to honestly share what had happened to them and how they felt about it, a decision that turned them into human beings. They were no longer flat characters to each other—party hacks toeing the party line—but round characters with complex motives, complicated thoughts, and vulnerable feelings, reacting to a situation none of them thought possible in our democracy.

Nothing kills curiosity more than turning others into caricatures; nothing nurtures it more than sharing the fullness of our humanity with one another, frailties, faults, and all. The stories these members shared cultivated the curiosity they needed to understand one another and to retrieve their better selves. As Ripley recounts:

> Afterward, several members told Kilmer they were ready to work together. Nothing was resolved, but much was illuminated. "It was still pretty raw," Timmons says, "but it was helpful to understand the degree to which [some members] were legitimately in fear for their lives. It made me understand where they were coming from."

That understanding was just enough for the committee to get back to work. It took some time, but sitting side by side and talking directly with one another allowed a bruised team to work together toward a common goal.

Putting Congress to work for the people

The fifty-year trend toward greater ideological cohesion within parties and greater ideological distance across them feeds on itself. The closer a party grows within, the further it moves away from the other party, a self-reinforcing cycle that makes it difficult for Congress to work for the people. "That's the thing about polarization. Sometimes once it gets started, it's hard to stop," observed Howard Rosenthal and Adam Bonica in a 2013 Reuters article on polarization in Congress.

Kilmer, Graves, and Timmons interrupted that dynamic in the select committee by doing things to intentionally disrupt it. They took that same approach to a number of their recommendations, in one instance, asking a sports coach how he had turned a toxic, loser team into a winning one and how they might do that in Congress.[161]

"Well, I don't know anything about Congress," the coach demurred.

"I don't want to ask you about Congress," Kilmer pressed. "I want to know what you do when players on your team are actively trying to sabotage the team."

That led to a back-and-forth on different options used by sport teams to build a winning culture. After eliminating firing and benching, the coach asked Kilmer what they did for those first entering Congress. "It's funny you ask," Kilmer answered. "When you show up for Freshman Orientation, they say, 'Democrats, you get on this bus; Republicans, you get on that bus.' And most of the orientation is designed to keep the two parties apart, and that sets the tone for the rest of their time here."

"Well, Derek," the coach said, "I don't know much about Congress, but it seems to me like you ought to stop doing that."

So that is what the committee did. It recommended that all incoming Democrats and Republicans be brought together, not separated, so they could get to know one another as people.

A second recommendation speaks to Woody Allen's observation that 99 percent of life is just showing up. Sometimes it is *impossible* for legislators to show up for committee meetings, or if they do show up, to stay for more than a few minutes before running off to the next meeting. "That's really good for cardio, but really bad for legislating," Kilmer quipped. Timmons points out that members of Congress are usually triple scheduled all the time, making it hard to learn anything or to accomplish much. "The more time we can be engaging in dialogue

---

[161] This account is based on Patton's interview cited earlier.

and understanding the issues," says Kilmer, "the better off we're going to be and the better off the American people will be." To make that possible, they orchestrated the creation of a tool to "deconflict" their schedules. "If middle schools can 'deconflict' their schedules, so can we."

Although the committee made over 200 recommendations, my first thought upon hearing these two was, "Where's the beef?" Then I realized that, like the committee's operating procedures, these two recommendations were targeting the culture of Congress. They were designed to close the distance between parties and to open the space within them so they could increase collaboration, reduce dysfunction, and make more progress. If they worked anywhere near as well as the committee's operating procedures, they would be Grade A Wagyu beef.

Be the change you want to see

While political commentators often look back wistfully at the 1950s through the 1970s as the golden age of bipartisanship, those three decades were more the exception than the rule. Polarization in Congress is the historical norm.[162] As problematic as that fact is, it is not surprising. Since our inception as a nation, we have lived divided lives in groups significantly closer within than across, groups more likely to empathize with those inside and to fear those outside—a recipe, if ever there was one, for cooking up more polarization in Congress than not.

The Modernization Committee created a recipe for collaboration rather than polarization, so they could get things done for the American people. They bucked a historic and current trend, inside and outside of Congress, to bring committee members closer together so they could stop fighting and start learning from one another. They disagreed. They challenged each other. They confronted one another. "We had things we were passionate about that were really difficult to get done," said Timmons. "We sat there, and we worked through it. It was hard, but we figured out a way to achieve the objective."

The objective, by the way, was not "get my party to win and the other to lose." It was "get things done that matter to the people we serve." True collaboration, as opposed to faux collaboration, depends on confronting, not avoiding, differences; on creating constructive, not destructive, conflict; and most of all, on

---

[162] See, for example, Hahrie Han and David W. Brady, "A Delayed Return to Historical Norms: Congressional Party Polarization after the Second World War," *British Journal of Political Science,* vol. 37, no.3 (2007): 505–531.

putting differences and conflicts to work in the pursuit of an objective you share because you have defined it together.

> **Like all recipes, the recipe for that kind of collaboration has a predictable set of ingredients and proportions.**

You take people who are tired of being potted plants; you offer them an opportunity to make a difference; you then build mutual trust and respect by creating a physical, technological, and social space that opens the mental space within parties and closes the distance across them; finally, you let the resulting back-and-forth simmer until new ideas and options boil up to the surface, at which point you serve up something new, something people can use to improve the way things work in Congress.

"Relationships matter," Kilmer said, reflecting on his experience. "We approached each other from a position of trust, understanding that we weren't going to agree on everything, but agreeing that we would have some rules of engagement in which there would be no surprises and no efforts to make each other look bad. That's unique in Congress."

Timmons agreed. "It would have been very easy, especially given the challenges we faced over the last four years, to go back to our corners and fight. We did not do that. And that was very intentional, and it took leadership." *It took leadership.* Indeed, and not just from the chair and vice chair but from committee members as well.

What you and I can do to disrupt the triangle of doom

When I would tell colleagues and friends about RCI's work to "fix Congress," the first thing out of their mouths was not "That's *great!* How can I help?" It was "Good luck!"

At first, I found the response irritating. It was as if they saw no role for themselves, either in creating or in changing a reality they had just made hopeless by declaring it hopeless. Then I realized: *We have all turned into potted plants!*

Until we see an option better than sitting on a shelf waiting to get watered, until we see a way to make a difference like those on the select committee did, what else should I expect?

That's when I decided to write this book. I wanted people to know that, despite the largely defeatist, sensationalist approach of twenty-four-hour cable

TV and social media, there are plenty of options out there for making a difference with all sorts of people in all sorts of places. All you have to do is get off the shelf and join them. ***Full speed ahead. Cynicism be damned!***

What the Modernization Committee did, how they did it, and what they accomplished is something any committee in Congress can do. With support and encouragement from us, as citizens, undoubtedly more will. It does not take legislation or formal reform to pave the way first; we can pave the way for legislation and reform. What is to stop a motivated group of citizens from meeting with a receptive group of representatives on a common objective? Say, increasing collaboration and reducing polarization both in communities and in Congress.

Award-winning political scientist Dr. Jane Mansbridge is at the forefront of those reimagining the relationship between representatives and constituents. Concerned that the representative system in many democratic countries is coming under increasing strain, Mansbridge proposed an alternative in which representatives and citizens come closer together to listen to each other and to share their experiences, updating and revising their views in light of what they learn from listening to one another in a conversation based on mutual respect, not coercion or manipulation.[163] In calling this alternative model "aspirational," Mansbridge seems to understand how unrealistic the idea may strike so many of us.

Then again, if we tried it . . .

> **Who knows? Perhaps we could gradually reverse the triangle of doom by creating a triangle of progress between citizens, elected officials like Kilmer, Timmons, and Graves, and journalists interested in solutions, not just problems—like those you will meet in Essay 19.**

More surprising things have happened in our nation's history when we set our minds to it. We have no reason to believe we cannot surprise future generations. Lord knows, they are depending on us to do exactly that.

---

[163] This summary is an oversimplification of an important idea well-articulated in "Recursive Representation in the Representative System," *Harvard Kennedy School Working Paper*, Number RWP17-045, November 2017.

SIXTEEN

PUTTING FAITH
in
FRIENDSHIP

During my senior year in high school, my social studies teacher, Mr. Schuler, held a mock United Nations exercise. I got to be Yugoslavia. As conflict expert Peter Coleman would predict, once I was assigned to Team Yugoslavia, I felt great affection, even loyalty, toward the country and a good deal of respect for its president, Josip Broz Tito, whom I got to play. I especially admired Tito's efforts to forge a multiethnic community with widespread intermarriage and integrated housing. But as a rebellious teenager, it was his moxie toward Soviet Premier Josef Stalin that most captured my imagination. Immediately following World War II, the two leaders continually wrestled over how independent from the Soviet Union Yugoslavia got to operate. At the height of their conflict, Stalin sent several assassins to kill Tito. In response, Tito sent Stalin a letter. "Stop sending people to kill me," he ordered. "We've already captured five of them, one of them with a bomb and another with a rifle. . . . If you don't stop sending killers, I'll send one to Moscow, and I won't have to send a second."[164] In 1949, Yugoslavia broke free from the Soviet orbit, exiting its satellite system and launching the Non-Aligned Movement.

Forty years later, ten years after Tito's death and shortly after the breakup of the Soviet Union, I was saddened to see Yugoslavia collapse and its four major ethnic groups—the Serbs (Orthodox Christians), the Croats (Catholics), the Bosniaks (Muslims), and the ethnic Albanians (also Muslims)—descend into war stoked by latent ethnic tensions.

---

[164] Roy Medvedev, *The Unknown Stalin,* 2004, cited in Wikipedia's biography of Tito, https://rb.gy/y0u1o.

The American ambassador to Yugoslavia at the time, Warren Zimmermann, had a front-row seat to the country's demise. In an especially eerie paragraph in a 1995 *Foreign Affairs* article, he distilled what he learned:

> The breakup of Yugoslavia is a classic example of nationalism from the top down—a manipulated nationalism . . . The manipulators condoned and even provoked local ethnic violence in order to engender animosities that could then be magnified by the press, leading to further violence . . . Nationalist "intellectuals," wrapped in the mantle of august academies of sciences, expounded their pseudo-history of the victimization of Serbs (or Croats) through the ages . . . Worst of all, the media, under the thumb of most republican regimes, spewed an endless daily torrent of violence and enmity. As a reporter for Vreme, one of the few independent magazines left in the former Yugoslavia, said, "You Americans would become nationalists and racists too if your media were totally in the hands of the Ku Klux Klan."[165]

The modern-day shots heard round the world

As far away in time and space as present-day Pittsburgh is from Yugoslavia in the early 1990s, the antisemitic mass murder of eleven Jews at Pittsburgh's Tree of Life synagogue in October 2018 evokes that earlier time and distant place, complete with nationalist manipulators, aided and abetted by a far-right media pitting race against race and religion against religion.

Pittsburgh sits in the southwest corner of a battleground state in the eastern part of the United States, a stone's throw from Ohio in the Midwest and from West Virginia in the South. Like a number of cities in the East, my hometown of Boston among them, it is known for its historic love of liberty and its historic practice of segregating demographic groups into different neighborhoods. Most Black families in Pittsburgh live in the Hill District, most Jewish families in Squirrel Hill, most upper-crust White families in the mostly Catholic Shadyside neighborhood, and so on. Divided by the Allegheny, Monongahela, and Ohio rivers, Pittsburgh is known as the City of Bridges, with 446 bridges connecting its geographically and demographically divided neighborhoods.

Into the kindling of such divides, hate groups have been tossing one match after another in the hope of turning a failed melting pot into a toxic cauldron.

---

[165] Warren Zimmermann, "The Last Ambassador: A Memoir of the Collapse of Yugoslavia." Originally published by *Foreign Affairs* in March 1995, *Foreign Affairs* republished it in their *Summer Reads* newsletter on August 8, 2023.

Since 1999, the U.S. has seen a 55 percent rise in these hate groups, with a brief decline during Obama's presidency followed by a sharp incline during Trump's. The vast majority of these groups adhere to some form of white supremacist ideology, as do many nationalists. "Nationalism is by nature uncivil, undemocratic, and separatist," wrote Zimmermann of the rising nationalism in Yugoslavia as it was imploding, "because it empowers one ethnic group over all others." By 2018, the year of the Tree of Life attack, White nationalist groups had jumped from 100 to 148 nationwide, an increase that drove uncivil discourse, undemocratic actions, and separatist talk deep into the public culture.[166] Three months after the attack, Southern Poverty Law Center's president, Richard Cohen, noted how hate was fraying the social fabric of our country.

Table 16.1: The Rise of Hate Groups[167]

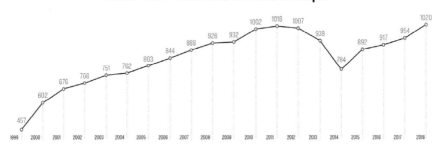

> "Knitting [our social fabric] back together will take the efforts of all segments of our society—our families, our schools, our houses of worship, our civic organizations and the business community."

At the forefront of those efforts are the citizens of Pittsburgh and the national, citizen-led organization Not In Our Town (NIOT), founded after the PBS film of the same name. In the wake of the deadliest antisemitic attack in the history of the United States, NIOT's founder and independent filmmaker, Patrice O'Neill, and her filmmaking team went to Pittsburgh to document the city's response to hate, as they had earlier gone to Billings, Montana.[168] The result is *Repairing the*

[166] Robert Hariman, "Public Culture," December 2016: "public culture refers most broadly to the dynamic negotiation of beliefs, values, and attitudes regarding collective association through media and other social practices that are defined by norms of open access and voluntary response." For more, go to https://rb.gy/b5hoo.

[167] "Hate Groups Reach Record High," SPLC Report, February 19, 2019.

[168] See Essay 10: "Taking a Stand."

World, a documentary that follows Pittsburghers over three years as they picked up the shards of their collective trauma and used them to build hundreds of relational bridges across lines of difference, showing those who would harm them: "We are stronger than hate."

Repairing the World tells a story that is at once devastating, moving, inspiring, and most of all, necessary. It opens with David Shribman of the *Pittsburgh-Post Gazette*: "I didn't hear the shots the first time. I hear them all the time now . . . So many of us, whether Jewish or not—whether from Squirrel Hill or not, whether in Pittsburgh that morning or not—hear those shots still. They were the modern-day shots heard round the world in our contemporary crisis of hurt and hate."[169]

An ugly day in the neighborhood

Squirrel Hill is known as a quiet neighborhood, home to the late Fred Rogers, host of a children's educational program called *Mister Rogers' Neighborhood*. His show lasted thirty-three tumultuous years, beginning in 1968 during the civil rights and anti-war movements and lasting until 2001, the year of the 9/11 attacks. The power of friendship, so well exemplified by Fred Rogers, would prove essential to his hometown after October 27, 2018.

On that day, an unassuming, overweight, slightly graying forty-six-year-old man entered the Tree of Life synagogue and opened fire with an assault rifle and three semiautomatic pistols. A few days before, Columbia University and the Anti-Defamation League had each reported an increase in antisemitic postings on Twitter and Instagram.[170] On the morning of the attack, the shooter himself had posted a message on the web: "I can't stand by and watch my people get slaughtered," he wrote. "Screw your optics, I'm going in." By the time the assailant surrendered to the police, eighty-three minutes after entering the building, he had killed eleven of the twenty-two people in the building and wounded six, some old enough to have survived the Holocaust. In the intervening time, police overheard him say, "All these Jews need to die."

Twenty-two people from three congregations were preparing for worship that day. Among them were Andrea Wedner and her mother, Rose Mallinger, 97. Every Saturday Wedner and her mother would join others for Shabbat Saturday

---

[169] From *Repairing the World: Stories from the Tree of Life*, a film and community engagement project. https://repairingtheworldfilm.org.

[170] David Ingram, "Attacks on Jewish people rising on Instagram and Twitter, researchers say," NBC News, October 27, 2018, https://rb.gy/mnuit; Annabelle Timsit, "The Pittsburgh shooting is the culmination of an increase in anti-Semitism in the US," Quartz, October 27, 2018, https://rb.gy/3ujjp.

morning service at the Tree of Life, where each week Rose would read the prayer for peace.[171]

Wedner heard what sounded like a high shriek, then gunshots in the hallway outside the Pervin Chapel in the Tree of Life building.

"My mother looked at me and said, 'What do we do?' in a very scared voice," Wedner recalled in her testimony at the attacker's trial.

"My mother couldn't have run, and we didn't know if there were other people shooting."

She then saw the shooter standing toward the back of the chapel, not far from where she and her mother were hiding under their pew, lying head-to-head.

"I saw a white male with light-colored or gray hair, with a light-colored jacket," Wedner said, "and he was holding a big, long gun . . . I was frantic. I was scared as scared could be."

Wedner watched as the man stepped closer and shot her and her mother.

"I saw my right arm get blown open in two places," Wedner testified. Her mother was shot so badly Wedner doubted she could survive. After the shooter moved on, Wedner stayed where she was rather than leave her mother for a safer spot. When the SWAT officers finally came to escort her out of the building, she kissed her fingers and touched them to her mother's skin. "Mommy," she cried, then left for the hospital, where her husband finally found her. "I think Bubbe is gone," she sobbed.

By evening, news stations reported that along with Rose Mallinger, the shooter had killed Joyce Fienberg, 75; Richard Gottfried, 65; Daniel Stein, 71; Melvin Wax, 87; Irving Younger, 69; Dr. Jerry Rabinowitz, 66; the couple Bernice, 84, and Sylvan Simon, 86; and the brothers Cecil, 59, and David Rosenthal, 54.

Afterward, ProPublica reporter A.C. Thompson said of the attack, "It was horrifying. It was horrible, but it wasn't at all surprising to me. Since 2015, I've been studying the resurgence of white supremacist activity in the United States." While many discounted the proliferation of their social media threats and rage, Thompson took them seriously. "There's just this onslaught of antisemitism and it's all bound up in this resurgent white power movement."[172]

---

[171] Based on Wedner's trial testimony as reported by Toby Tabachnick, "Prosecution rests in first phase of synagogue massacre trial," *Pittsburgh Jewish Chronicle,* June 14, 2023.

[172] Unless otherwise noted, the material for the remainder of this essay comes from a transcript of the documentary *Repairing the World.* I have edited some quotes for brevity.

Five years later, the shooter, a "fringe figure in the online world of white supremacist rage," was found guilty and sentenced to death.[173]

The day you realize you're neighbors

The day and night of the attack, spontaneous outpourings of support spread throughout the city. Wasi Mohamed, a member of the Islamic Center of Pittsburgh, was among the first to reach out. "We offered to do anything the Jewish community needed," he recalled. "If it's standing in front of their services and protecting them, if it's buying groceries, if it's showing up for every funeral and Shiva." Whatever they needed, he told them, his center would be there.

High school students organized a gathering at Forbes and Murray Avenues in Squirrel Hill on the evening of the attack. Hundreds of people from across Pittsburgh showed up, clustered together, holding candles, a few playing music and singing, others standing silently, almost everyone holding on to one another, many of them crying. A young woman standing at the front of the gathering stepped forward and spoke into a microphone, "I am a different Jew today than I was yesterday."

No one in Pittsburgh was the same as they were the day before. "Pittsburgh has always been a city divided by race and class exacerbated by literal rivers," *Pittsburgh Post-Gazette* columnist Tony Norman said. "For the first time in my memory, so many neighborhoods coming together, shoulder to shoulder, mourning together, weeping in each other's arms, we realized that we were neighbors on that awful day."

Redefining what it means to be a neighbor

"The tragedy was like a death in our family. It occurs and everybody has a flurry of activity," said David Shribman of the *Pittsburgh Post-Gazette*. "Then thump, the activity is over, and the reckoning with the depth of the problem begins. How

---

[173] The descriptor "fringe figure" comes from Lois Beckett, "Pittsburgh shooter was fringe figure in online world of white supremacist rage," *Guardian,* October 30, 2018.

do we deal with this as a society? How do we deal with the few who are intent on causing harm and hatred for the many?"

Wasi Mohamed knows a lot about the depth of the problem. "Something that is always in the back of my mind any time I am at prayers on a Friday is something could happen. The Muslim community is no stranger to this kind of hatred."

Journalist Tony Norman could relate. "To be a Black newspaper columnist in Pittsburgh is to be well acquainted with hate in this region. There's a lot of it, and it isn't acknowledged nearly enough. It is not an abstraction to me. It comes to me before dawn in the form of calls to my office phone, usually a string of racial epithets let loose on the world like a scabrous jazz solo."

In recent years, that scabrous solo has been accompanied by a cable news chorus oozing hateful talk 24/7. At the time of the mass shooting, Fox News Channel and Fox and Friends commentators were routinely venting their spleens:

"People are coming into our country *illegally*."

"That's an *invasion*. It's not a caravan. It's an *invasion*."

"And the angry mob that's coming."

"Individuals are invading our country, and *something needs to be done about it*."

In his research, PublicSource journalist Richard Lord discovered that the attacker had dropped out of the real world and into a virtual one, leaving a digital trail of his "descent into this world of antisemitic conspiracy theories and anti-immigrant sentiment that was becoming more and more a part of the normal political discourse in 2017 and 2018." When that discourse began calling immigrants "invaders," a soon-to-be-mass-murderer took to social media to post his reaction: "I have noticed a change in people saying 'illegals' that now say 'invaders,' I like this."

Wasi Mohamed knew that a problem this deep and widespread would require them to do more than just support one another in vigils. To the few seeking to harm the many, they would have to prove that they were "stronger than hate," as Pittsburghers put it. To Rabbi Ron Symons of the Center for Loving Kindness, that meant redefining what it means to be a neighbor:

> **"It's not just about someone who lives next to you. A neighbor is someone who you actually have a moral responsibility towards and who has a moral responsibility towards you."**

Over the next months, as one national crisis after another swept the nation, Pittsburgh had plenty of chances to redefine the meaning of neighbor in terms of our moral responsibility toward one another.

In May 2020, a video was circulated nationwide, capturing Minneapolis police officer Derek Chauvin impassively kneeling on George Floyd's neck until he killed him. Tim Smith, the pastor of the Keystone Church in the Hazelwood neighborhood of Pittsburgh, called on his neighbors throughout Pittsburgh. "Right now, the house that's on fire are the houses of Black people. There are some things that we need to fix. We're going to have to combine our networks to get this job done." He then recounted, "I reached out to my clergy friends, my Jewish friends, saying 'come and stand with us so that we as the faith community can make a statement.'"

During the same time, Allderdice High School held discussions on antisemitism and racism in their civics classes. "It was an open dialogue with no judgment," one African American student said of the conversation. "That's important, especially for young people, because if you don't get that when you grow up, you're just back to self-segregation because you're not comfortable with people you normally wouldn't talk to."

Once the pandemic settled over the country and rumors of its origins spread misinformation and anti-Asian hate across the internet, the Asian American community came under threat. "For the Asian American community, the pandemic has been really, really hard," said Marian Lien of Pittsburgh's St. Edmunds Academy. "In a local market, I was told that I should be shipped off with the virus back to China. There's not one Asian American or one Asian immigrant right now who doesn't have that kind of a story." Only this time, neighbors showed up. "Within hours, our Jewish community immediately called me and said, 'Tell us what you need.'"

"What is happening to the country we call America? What is happening to our democracy?"

– Esther Bush, CEO, Urban League of Pittsburgh

In the years following the 2018 attack, neighbors reached out to neighbors across historic divides, again and again—and not just in crisis. They reflected together in citywide and national panels, at the Eradicate Hate Global Summit, in Congressional hearings, in city reports on the impact of gender and race.

In each case, they asked some form of the same question: *In a time of division, what will it take to stand together and stand up to hate? What can* you *do to stand up to hate?*

Building a better future out of relationships stronger than hate

Looking back, Wasi Mohamed summed up his experience: "The story of what happened starts with some of the worst pain you can imagine and ends with some of the best and closest relationships I could have ever hoped for."

Journalist Tony Norman had a similar experience. "The Tree of Life and George Floyd in a very horrific, ironic way made it possible for people to be vulnerable with each other. They forced people to cross bridges that they weren't comfortable crossing. And once people got into the habit of crossing bridges, you began to see a new spirit emerge." Later on, he adds, "It really does feel like something has changed. The metaphorical and literal bridges are being crossed."

So how did Pittsburghers manage to cross bridges so many in our nation fear to cross? "The goal of preventing hate and violence pulls people in," *Repairing the World* producer Patrice O'Neill told me in an interview. "It gets them working together, especially people who aren't in polarized camps." O'Neill has been using her documentaries to engage communities ever since the 1995 PBS film *Not In Our Town.* She sees her work as part of a movement among journalists to engage communities in the story-telling process, so they can create "restorative narratives" that help communities recover from the crises or disasters most news outlets just report. [174]

A consistent theme runs through O'Neill's work: the power generated by citizens when they come together and work toward a common goal. It is the kind of power generated by nuclear fusion rather than fission. Whereas fission splits one heavy, unstable nucleus into two lighter nuclei, fusion releases vastly greater amounts of energy by bringing two light nuclei together. [175] In her book *Civic*

---

[174] For more, see Essay 10: "Taking a Stand" and Essay 19: "Rewriting the News That's Fit to Print."

[175] "Fission vs. Fusion—What's the Difference?" Duke Energy Information Center, May 2021, https://rb.gy/eca3v.

Fusion, mediator extraordinaire Susan Podziba illustrates how even communities riven by divisive value conflict can come together through a process akin to fusion to achieve a common public policy goal.[176]

In Pittsburgh, the Tree of Life attack taught a lesson about fusion that we still have to learn as a nation. When you live separate lives in segregated communities, it is hard *not* to put your community's interests above all others, even when it undercuts your power as a citizen to create a better future. Jasiri X spoke to how he learned that lesson at an event that brought different communities together to reflect on what they learned from the Tree of Life attack: "I was in the Black community, and I was about Black issues. I now understand white supremacist violence is not just a Black or Brown issue; it's a Jewish issue as well. And if we're all under attack by this white supremacist violence, why shouldn't we be in solidarity?"

Where true safety lies

Wasi Mohamed believes the different communities across Pittsburgh can sustain the bonds they forged after the attack and build a more unified city, even a more unified country. It will no doubt take Fred Rogers' talent for friendship and his ability to bond with a wide range of people of all ages and types. But if his hometown is any indication, that rare ability and talent can be forged most quickly and deeply in the heat of the moment when necessity requires it, when, as Norman put it, ***people are forced to cross bridges until they get in the habit of crossing bridges.***

Wasi Mohamed put it this way: "True safety is not going to be through having weapons. It is going to be through changing the sentiment in this country, and relationships are the foundation on which all of that is built. I'm looking for a place that has people I know I can stand with, that will dig the trenches with me, and prepare for anything that's coming, together. Pittsburgh's that place."

Like all of us, the people of Pittsburgh just want to be safe. After witnessing the Tree of Life massacre, every instinct is telling them to seek that safety in relationships, not guns.

The story of Yugoslavia's descent into inter-ethnic conflict and war, driven by a

> "Ensuring these **relationships grow**, that is the way we truly become **stronger than hate.**"
> — Wasi Mohamed

---

[176] Susan Podziba, *Civic Fusion: Mediating Polarized Public Dispute* (American Bar Association, 2013). For examples, go to https://www.podziba.com/projects.

campaign of nationalist propaganda that too few resisted, is a cautionary tale. By the time all was said and done, the Yugoslav Wars became the deadliest armed conflict in Europe since World War II, resulting in somewhere between 130,000 to 140,000 deaths, the largest refugee and humanitarian crisis in European history, and war crimes that included genocide, crimes against humanity, and mass wartime rape.

If we do not resist these same divisive nationalist efforts in our own country, if we let the tight insular space within groups and the gaping distance across groups devolve into violence, we will likely go the way of Yugoslavia. If we choose instead to redefine the space between us by opening the space within our own groups and closing the distance among them—as so many in Pittsburgh did—we can repair the world and build a better future together.

After the Tree of Life massacre, sixteen-year-old Peyton Klein founded the Global Minds Initiative to move the world in that direction. The attack convinced her that nothing is more important or more powerful than creating a sense of belonging and community:

> "*Tikkun olam* is a Hebrew concept. It means *to repair the world, to make the world a better place.* While we are not required to complete the task, we are not absolved from trying."

The story continues . . .

The story of Pittsburgh, repeated for centuries across our nation and around the world, is not over. Hamas's massacre of Israeli citizens in the name of Palestinian liberation, just three weeks before the fifth anniversary of the Tree of Life massacre, opened old wounds and resurrected old divisions. In Pittsburgh, Tree of Life rabbi and survivor Jeffrey Meyers was disappointed that those who had reached out to him and his congregation after the 2018 massacre did not reach out after the Hamas attack on Israel. Nor, apparently, did he reach out to them, although they too might have been hurting after Israel's counterattack.

In Germany, where the shadow of the Holocaust still hangs over the nation's conscience, most Germans sided with the Israelis.[177] In the United States, where the shadow of slavery hangs over ours, many on the American left sided with the Palestinians subjugated in Israel much like African-Americans are in the U.S.

---

[177] Susan Neiman, "Germany on Edge." *New York Review of Books.* November 3, 2023.

Then the question is: What role will you and I play in this cyclical story of hate and violence?

> **Will we retreat to our own groups, take sides, and become co-conspirators, or will we seek to interrupt the cycle by resisting the hate that hate evokes?**

On October 25, 2023—two weeks after the Hamas attack, in the midst of Israel's counterattack, and two days before the fifth anniversary of the Tree of Life massacre—Robyn Sue Fisher of San Francisco chose love after someone smashed the front windows of her ice cream shop and spray painted "Free Palistin" (sic) on its storefront. Fisher is Jewish. No other nearby stores were targeted. The police are treating it as a hate crime.[178]

"At first, I felt fear, and then I felt anger, and then I felt a deep sorrow," Fisher said. "And then I felt empathy, and that's how I got to love."

Fisher wrote an open letter to the community. "This is a defining moment for us," she wrote, "as a community, as leaders, and as parents of children who are watching us and learning from our actions. We cannot choose how others treat us, but we can choose how we respond. I CHOOSE LOVE. Now more than ever."

As a part of that choice, Fisher decided to create a new line of T-shirts and sweatshirts that say, "In the spirit of ice cream, I choose LOVE." Proceeds will go not to her pockets but to San Francisco's Courage Museum, set to open in 2025 and dedicated to "ending the public health crisis caused by violence and the hate that fuels it."

Fisher's choice sparked a new cycle—one of love and support. Since she posted her open letter on her storefront and on her Instagram site, Fisher has received an overwhelming number of messages from friends and strangers alike. One came from another San Francisco small business owner, a Palestinian American. "My support to you," he wrote. "No one that does that speaks for Palestinians . . . We are feeling unsafe as well and afraid to speak up. There's love here. I choose that." So too have many others. A GoFundMe campaign, launched by friends, has already raised $70,000 to cover the store's repairs and her employees' lost wages.

"I'm more committed to keeping [Smitten Ice Cream] open than ever," Fisher said. "I want to offer a message of resilience and love." And if she met the

---

[178] This account is based on Heather Knight, "San Francisco Shop Owner Responds to Hate Crime With Message of Love." *New York Times*. Nov. 6, 2023.

person who attacked her store? Easy: "I would invite them to have some ice cream with me."[179]

The next and last essay in Part 4 is perhaps the most challenging, because it goes to the heart of our struggle, as a people and as a nation, to resist and even transform the hate that hate evokes. Few understand this better than Dan Leger. He was there the day a man full of hate attacked the Tree of Life and took from him the lives of people he loved. "Here is the hardest part," he said afterward, "to learn to listen and to communicate and to help those who live in the prison of hate and isolation and bitterness and fear and to somehow learn to move beyond 'I am right and you are wrong.'" The next essay offers insight into how.

---

[179] Heather Knight, "San Francisco Shop Owner Responds to Hate Crime With Message of Love." *New York Times*. Nov. 6, 2023.

SEVENTEEN

BEFRIENDING YOUR IDEOLOGICAL ENEMY

In 2011, the student body at Florida's New College discovered that a White nationalist was living in their midst, attending courses right alongside them. They were outraged. Everything about White nationalism was abhorrent to this mostly White, liberal student body, many of whom were social justice activists. Much to their horror, they knew that White nationalism had been gaining steady ground over three decades, transforming itself in the public eye from a violent extremist group into a user-friendly, mainstream political force orchestrated by now-fellow student Derek Black's godfather, former Ku Klux Klan grand wizard David Duke, and Derek's father, Don Black, founder of the White national-ist website Stormfront.[180] As soon as news of Derek spread, the students' online message board, the *forum*, lit up, calling for his expulsion or ostracism. Anyone advocating otherwise was considered naïve at best and conspiring with the enemy at worst. It was obvious. Derek was an "idiot," "a hate monger," "a Hitler," "a fraud." "You simply cannot reason with someone like that."

Disrupting the status quo by creating a context of belonging

A small, diverse group of friends saw things differently. Each of them lived on the periphery of the school's culture, far enough away from its left-leaning cen-ter to resist its pugnacious pull. Instead of pushing Derek away, they made a

---

[180] Most of this account is based on Eli Saslow's remarkable book, *Rising Out of Hatred* (New York: Doubleday, 2019).

111

different, unexpected choice. They chose to bring Derek closer, inviting him to join them for dinner on Friday evening to celebrate Shabbat. When Derek, a self-avowed antisemite, accepted, several regulars dropped out in protest. But Shabbat host Matthew Stephenson was adamant. "Just don't be assholes," he told those remaining. "We want him to come back."

Matthew saw no purpose in directly confronting Derek's beliefs. He knew Derek was a smart debater, accustomed to making rational arguments and fending off challenges. He knew Derek had been homeschooled by his White nationalist family, surrounded by his White nationalist community, as far away from Jews and people of color as they could manage. Matthew understood that nothing he or anyone said during one dinner would ever shake, let alone change, Derek's worldview. So instead of trying to build a case, Matthew decided to build a relationship, one in which Derek could learn for himself what the "enemy" was actually like.[181]

For months, this unlikely group broke bread together, drank wine, discussed world religion, and got to know one another independent of their different beliefs. Among this group was Juan Elias, a Peruvian immigrant who had met Derek on the first day of school. As the two became friends, Juan noticed in Derek things only a friend could notice, like Derek's gentle kindness and intense curiosity. When Juan learned of Derek's White nationalist allegiance, he looked beyond the White nationalist label to his experience of Derek as a friend, deciding not to shun him, even though Derek had advocated deporting immigrants like him on Stormfront. Matthew Stephenson, one of the only Orthodox Jews on campus, had met Derek the first week of school, as Derek strummed his guitar and sang country-and-western songs in one of the school's courtyards. Guided by a Kabbalah faith that instructed its followers to seek the best in people, Matthew decided to invite Derek to his home for Shabbat dinner. Moshe Ashe agreed to cohost, despite his Jewish grandfather barely surviving the Holocaust after Nazis imprisoned him in the Bergen-Belsen concentration camp. He brought the weight of that legacy to his relationship with Derek. In *Rising Out of Hatred,* Eli Saslow recounts how Moshe somehow "found it in himself to befriend Derek, to invite him over for beers, to join him at Shabbat dinners, and to sometimes speak with him in the German they had both decided to learn because of their divergent family legacies."[182]

---

[181] Ibid., 81.

[182] Ibid., 158.

In this anything but random act of kindness, Matthew and his friends lifted their gaze to what stands before them, not between them.[183] They could easily have made a different choice. They could have gone along with their peers on the student message board, pressuring them to reject not only Derek's views but the man himself. Derek could have retreated to his family's home and sought affirmation from his White nationalist community. These are the predictable choices, the automatic choices most of us make.

Instead, they forged a new way through the thicket they had inherited from generations before them. They created a context of belonging, and in that context, they stood their ground and eventually changed the ground upon which they stood.

Putting conflict to work

The last person to befriend Derek was Matthew's roommate, Allison Gornick, a White woman from a small Midwest town, who thought Matthew's efforts with Derek profoundly misguided. Every Friday, she would go to her room and shut the door in protest. But over the next year, she and Derek gradually became friends—first by chance, when they found themselves together on a friend's boat, then by choice, when Allison grew more and more curious about how someone who seemed so mild and kind could promote something so hateful and oppressive. "I'm wicked curious about the kid," she wrote a friend. "I'm like a detective."[184]

Unlike the others befriending Derek, Allison's curiosity fueled a mounting determination to understand Derek's beliefs, not avoid them. When Allison first asked Derek if they could talk about his beliefs, Derek dreaded the idea. He hated tension with those close to him, and up until then, no one close to him had ever challenged his beliefs. But when he realized it might help him learn how to disarm liberals, he told her to go ahead.

As the two went back and forth confronting one another's beliefs, they quickly discovered that they both relished debate. They enjoyed hashing out diametrically opposed views. They welcomed new facts; they loved challenging each other's interpretations of those facts; and they were intrigued by points of view they had never heard in their own like-minded groups.

---

[183] As Amanda Gorman put it in her poem, "The Hill We Climb," recited at the 2020 Presidential Inauguration, rb.gy/myq29.

[184] Ibid., 118.

> **As one debate gave way to another, a distinct form of dialogue and friendship emerged, one grounded in facts, nurtured by curiosity, and focused on learning.**

In this unusual context of belonging they created together, Allison came to see that Derek was not the stereotypical White nationalist she had imagined him to be, and she realized how little she knew about the issues White nationalists put at the center of their ideology. Derek came to see that Allison was not the biased, ill-informed, liberal enemy he had expected. "For years Derek had been hearing about the abstract evils of racism, which he had always dismissed as empty rhetoric from his enemies on the liberal left," recounts Saslow. "But he didn't consider Allison an enemy, so now he spent hours on his computer reading through raw data, doing his own research, and debating the evidence with Allison."[185]

In each of their many debates, they adhered to one unspoken rule, intuitively understanding that it would yield more learning than would abandoning it:

> **Follow the evidence and explore what it means with people whose views and life experiences are different from your own.**

This one rule separates people living in groups with an open mental space from those living in tight, insular ones, and it is increasingly rare in our polarized, pluralist nation. By taking the risk of becoming friends in a world unfriendly to cross-ideological friendships, they were able to engage in debates that uncovered new facts and exposed old falsehoods, allowing both of them to assess the world for themselves. In this respect, their friendship offers a model for all of us hoping to protect a democracy struggling under the weight of faux facts and grand falsehoods. "Democracy and nationhood depend on the capacity of individuals to assess the world for themselves and take unexpected risks," says tyranny expert Timothy Snyder; "their destruction depends on asserting grand falsehoods that are known to be such."[186]

Combining empathy with accountability

As essential as such friendships may be to democracy, they are not easy. Almost two years into their friendship, now a romantic relationship, Derek read an

---

[185] Ibid., 168.

[186] Timothy Snyder, "Ukraine Holds the Future: The War Between Democracy and Nihilism," *Foreign Affairs,* September/October 2022.

especially hurtful thread on *the forum* while they were both traveling. He texted Allison: "I understand there are intellectual ideas to discuss," he vented, "and yet I feel almost betrayed." Allison could empathize. Derek had just posted a message on *the forum*, clarifying his changing views in an effort to reassure his fellow students. Their skeptical, hostile reactions hurt him. A common "supportive" response to such hurt is to take your friend's side and agree with them. Allison's support was radically different. She wrote back:

> For them, what you believe in are not simply 'intellectual ideas.' They are abhorrent and dangerous. And to them, it's not just that you believe it . . . It's that you publicly believe these things. And in that, you're *distanced* from them. You're not a classmate. You're a public figure. Your vulnerabilities and emotions don't necessarily matter to them. It's not like you haven't done anything that reinforces and spreads the WN ideology—you have. To them you are not a victim—and in general you aren't because, to be frank, you absolutely have done all those things. They hurt you, yes. Because in their view your public beliefs oppress and hurt others, and yeah, I agree with them. I don't think there is a nice way to say that.[187]

Wow. As Allison says, there is no easy way to say that. There are, however, more or less helpful ways, and in her response, Allison helps Derek see what he cannot see from the *inside out* that she *can* see from the *outside in*: his impact and what he did to create it. This line of sight, hidden from him and available to Allison, gives Derek his best chance of learning and growing.

Derek took it. Over the next weeks, Derek reflected on what Allison said in light of the research he continued to do on his own. It finally hit him. His friends at the Shabbat dinners—Matthew worrying about wearing a yarmulke in the South, Juan sleeping in the gym to save money for tuition, Moshe knowing his grandfather barely survived the Holocaust—were the ones suffering discrimination. "How didn't I see some of this stuff before?" he asked Allison. "When you look at the numbers, it's pretty clear." A few weeks later, he wrote Allison again. "I'm done," he said. "I don't believe in it, and I'm not going to be involved."[188] Soon after, he publicly disavowed White nationalism in a public letter to the Southern Poverty Law Center.

Afterward, Derek receded into anonymity for a while, declining requests for interviews. His one public response was to the *Daily Beast*, which had published an article on his transformation that overlooked its most important catalyst. He wrote:

---

[187] Saslow, 2019, 199. My emphasis.

[188] Ibid., 202–203. My emphasis.

People who disagreed with me were critical in this process. Especially those who are my *friends regardless,* but who let me know when we talked about it that they thought my beliefs were wrong and took the time to provide evidence and civil arguments. I didn't always agree with their ideas, but I listened to them and they listened to me.

Furthermore, a critical juncture was when I realized that *a friend was considered an outsider by the philosophy I supported. It's a huge contradiction* to share your summer plans with someone whom you completely respect, only to then realize that your ideology doesn't consider them a full member of society. *I couldn't resolve that.*[189]

The transformational power of friendship

In the end, despite the disruption to his identity, the loss of his future as a movement leader, and the pain of alienating his family, Derek resolved to live "in the truth," as Václav Havel once put it. That choice was made possible by "friends regardless," friends who openly disagreed with his beliefs, who looked at the evidence with him, who listened to him and to whom he listened. It was the connective tissue of these friendships that allowed these students to reach across the ideological distance between them and sustain that connection long enough for the distance between them to grow closer and for transformation to occur.

In November 2016, shortly after 74.2 million voters made Donald Trump president of the United States, Derek Black published an article in the *New York Times.*[190] I quote it at length below and recommend it in its entirety. It is Exhibit A in the case for the transformational power of friendships across divides.

> I could easily have spent the night of Nov. 8 elated, surrounded by friends and family, thinking: "We did it. We rejected a multicultural and globalist society. We defied the elites, rejected political correctness, and made a statement millions of Americans have wanted to shout for decades."
>
> I'd be planning with other white nationalists what comes next, and assessing just how much influence our ideology would have on this administration. That's who I was a few years ago.
>
> Things look very different for me now. I am far away from the community that I grew up in, and that I once hoped could lead our country to a moment like this. . . .

---

[189] Ibid., 225. My emphasis.

[190] R. Derek Black, "Why I Left White Nationalism," *New York Times,* November 26, 2016. My emphasis.

Several years ago, I began attending a liberal college where my presence prompted huge controversy. *Through many talks with devoted and diverse people there—people who chose to invite me into their dorms and conversations rather than ostracize me—I began to realize the damage I had done. Ever since, I have been trying to make up for it. . . .*

People have approached me looking for a way to change the minds of Trump voters, but I can't offer any magic technique. That kind of persuasion happens in person-to-person interactions and it requires a lot of honest listening on both sides. . . .

I have no doubt that many [Trump] supporters voted thinking he'd soften his rhetoric, that his words didn't really matter. The words were not disqualifying for them because they don't see, or refuse to see, what the message of hate will reap. . . .

Even those on the furthest extreme of the white nationalist spectrum don't recognize themselves doing harm—I know that because it was easy for me, too, to deny it. . . .

Mr. Trump's victory must make all Americans acknowledge that the choice of embracing or rejecting multiculturalism is not abstract. I know this better than most, because I followed both paths. *It is the choice of embracing or rejecting our own people.*

PART 4

TURNING FORCES OF DIVISION

into

FORCES FOR GOOD

Freedom is a fragile thing and it's never more than one generation away from extinction. It is not ours by way of inheritance; it must be fought for and defended constantly by each generation.

—Ronald Reagan
Gubernatorial Inaugural Address, 1967

If you want to solve a problem, then you have to take in the whole truth. And you have to admit that nobody's hands are clean, that all of us are complicit to some degree.

—Barack Obama
Pod Save America, 2023

EIGHTEEN

MENDING
OUR FRAYED
SOCIAL FABRIC

In 2021, a year into a pandemic that closed businesses and opened old wounds, two knitting enthusiasts on opposite sides of the country called on volunteers to complete labors of love left undone by those who had died or fallen too ill to finish them.[191] Over a thousand people of all ages, religions, nationalities, and political affiliations answered that call, completing hundreds of knitting projects through Loose Ends.[192] Before knitting a stitch, each "finisher" first added a "lifeline," a thread sown into a row of knitted stitches to prevent the original design from unraveling. Only then did they pick up the work of someone no longer able to do so.

Our Founders left us an unfinished project: a democracy "conceived in liberty and dedicated to the proposition that all men are created equal," as President Lincoln put it in the Gettysburg Address on November 19, 1863. Just over two years earlier on July 4, 1861, Lincoln addressed Congress: "Our popular government has often been called an experiment. Two points in it our people have already settled: the successful establishing and the successful administering of it. One still remains: its successful maintenance against a formidable internal attempt to overthrow it."

---

[191] Caitlin Huson, "They died leaving labors of love undone. Strangers complete their work," *Washington Post,* February 8, 2023, rb.gy/iqjydl.

[192] looseendsproject.org

In those words, Lincoln defined the work that was left unfinished by those who came before him. "It is now for [us] to demonstrate to the world that those who can fairly carry an election can also suppress a rebellion; that ballots are the rightful and peaceful successors of bullets; and that when ballots have fairly and constitutionally decided, there can be no successful appeal back to bullets; that there can be no successful appeal except to ballots themselves, at succeeding elections." That was the work Lincoln, and those who stood with him, took on and completed before Lincoln was assassinated.

Today tens of thousands of citizens across the country are answering the call to pick up the unfinished project our Founders started and Lincoln continued. Together these citizens are mending a social fabric so frayed it risks falling apart. *In one way or another, they are all tending to the fabric's loose ends, those unsettled conflicts over who we are and want to be as a nation and a people.* And in one way or another, they are all sowing into that fabric a lifeline, so we can preserve our Founders' original design as we take up their unfinished work.

At Princeton's nonpartisan Bridging Divides Initiative (BDI), Nealin Parker spends her days tracking citizen groups working to reduce the polarization shredding our social fabric.[193] In 2022, she mapped seven thousand citizen groups and is still counting. The breadth of these efforts is stunning. Some are bridging partisan divides through constructive debate while building a citizen movement to reduce polarization. Others are helping people from different places, parties, and perspectives understand and empathize with one another. And still others are repairing relationships so riven by conflict they have broken down altogether.[194] Every day we hear or read countless stories in the news about how our country is falling apart. This essay tells stories about the people who are knitting it back together again.

Bridging partisan divides

In 2016, after one of the most corrosive elections in American history, three citizens—David Blankenhorn, Bill Doherty, and David Lapp—launched Braver Angels, an initiative sponsored by the Institute for American Values. They wanted to see if Americans could still *respectfully* disagree, maybe even find or create

---

[193] Bridging Divides Initiative, https://bridgingdivides.princeton.edu. Also see "Political polarization prompts efforts to bridge the gap through shared experiences," PBS NewsHour, January 10, 2022.

[194] Go to Citizen Connect at https://citizenconnect.us for information on over 500 organizations focused on everything from election reform to civic education to restoring civil dialogue. Also, see the list at the end of David Bornstein's article, "Restoring the (Lost) Art of Civility," *New York Times,* October 29, 2018, https://rb.gy/oznhte.

Figure 18.1: Groups Reducing Polarization across Our Nation

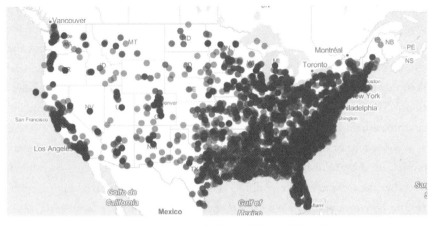

Source: Bridging Divides Initiative at Princeton University

common ground in the face of a growing post-election divide. After several gatherings of "Blues" and "Reds" showed that it was possible, Blankenhorn turned to building an organization that could bridge partisan divides across the nation. Since then, Braver Angels has grown in size and reputation. Every level of its leadership is equally balanced between conservatives and progressives, with "patriotic volunteers" working in communities, on college campuses, in the media, and in government to move the polarization dial from hatred or disdain to respect and appreciation, from "they are our enemy" to "they have something important to contribute." Their well-known debate program, designed by Alice Lawson, aims to build rather than destroy relationships by transforming traditional rules of debate into three rules that make it safe for even uncertain participants to engage:

- **Say what you truly believe:** Sincerity is disarming, so express the full extent of your passion along with your doubts.

- **Welcome every voice:** Give everyone equal time and listen to each argument in turn. View the debate not as a contest but as a collective search for the truth.

- **Address questions to the chair, not other participants,** so people are less likely to experience a question as an aggressive challenge.

When you structure debates this way, the results are surprising. "On immigration, racial justice, and other highly controversial topics, people are astonished to discover that *they mostly agree*," says Lawson. "And when common ground isn't established, the foundation is laid for genuine synthesis of the best in each side, which can generate not just awareness of shared humanity, but actual policy progress." Lawson has grown used to such results, but even she was surprised by an October 2020 debate on the election which affected how almost half the attendees said they would vote. Most meaningful to Lawson, however, is how the debates affect the way each side sees the other: "There is a restoration of awareness of the deep dignity of the other side."[195]

Since then, Braver Angels has taken off, as have their ambitions. In addition to their debate program, they now offer a slew of workshops and trainings on everything from how to become a debate chair, to how to reduce polarization, to how to talk constructively with people on the other side of a partisan divide. They send out emails regularly, outlining actions any one of us can take "to fix our nation." Most ambitious of all, early in 2023, they announced a campaign to build a civic-renewal movement called *Rise for America*, aimed at creating large-scale change by turning civic rancor into civic renewal across the country.[196]

Figure 18.2: The Changes Braver Angels Seek

1. Rising trust in one another as valued and welcome fellow citizens.

2. Rising trust in civic, religious, and governmental institutions.

3. More participation in voluntary associations.

4. More involvement in civic and political activities.

5. More Americans across the political spectrum believing that what unites us is more important than what divides us, that our democracy is working well, that Congress is doing a good job, and that the media are honest and fair-minded. And that higher education is working well.

Source: Rise for America Website

They launched the campaign at their third national convention in July 2023, fittingly held in Gettysburg, Pennsylvania. A *New York Times* journalist and editorial board member, Farah Stockman, attended the convention. Afterward, she reported

---

[195] Alice Lawson, "Building Trust Across the Political Divide: The surprising bridge of conflict," *Comment,* January 21, 2021. For online debates, go to https://braverangels.org/what-we-do/debates/. For more on how Braver Angels leads debates, go to https://drive.google.com/file/d/1ptJDWP5pjbhZQkcn-4PXyWBNRrrQUZk8U/view.

[196] To join the Rise for America campaign, go to https://braverangels.org/rise/.

on her experience, marveling at the hip-hop, bluegrass music the multiracial band, Gangstagrass, brought to the festivities. They were the right band at the right place at the right time. "Instead of pitting rural America against urban America," Stockman writes, "Gangstagrass tries to appeal to both at the same time."[197] She was struck by the positive energy that both Gangstagrass and the Braver Angels crowd exuded *and* by how much they went against the grain of current trends in America.

That, of course, is their point: to go against the grain of a divided, negative downward spiral. Only thing is, going against the grain makes both Gangstagrass and Braver Angels hard to place in our black-and-white, right-or-wrong, left-or-right taxonomy. As Stockman says, those who defy categories often go unseen. "Unless a news item fans the outrage of one side or the other," Stockman observes, "it risks falling through the cracks completely. Voters who defy categorization—we misfits who make up half of the American people—aren't well served by the process."[198]

And *that*, in a nutshell, is the problem Braver Angels is trying to solve. And those 50 percent of Americans who defy categorization? Braver Angels would love to reach them. So if you are among them, or even if you are not, sign up and join the merry band! There's a project that needs finishing, and America needs all the help she can get.

Understanding and empathizing with the "other side"

Some citizen-led groups are focusing less on the substantive differences driving us apart than on the misperceptions that turn those differences into "affective" polarization—what Larry Diamond calls the emotional, psychological, the 'I just hate the other side' kind of polarization.[199] This more emotional, relational approach brings members of different, often hostile groups together for an authentic experience, so they can better understand one another's views and empathize with their life experiences.[200] The goal of the approach is to dissipate fear and hate by disrupting the interlocking misperceptions that generate those reactions. Or to put it more positively, it is to help groups see one another in a new, more accurate light,

[197] Farah Stockman, "Opinion: This Is the Music America Needs," *New York Times*, August 5, 2023.

[198] Also see Mike Allen, "Record Number of Americans Say They are Politically Independent," *Axios*, April 17, 2023.

[199] As Larry Diamond put it in Talib Visram, "What happens when you put 926 random Americans in a room and tell them to solve the climate crisis," *Fast Company*, October 26, 2021.

[200] This approach is based loosely on a theory called the "contact hypothesis," an idea popularized in the 1950s by Gordon Allport, *The Nature of Prejudice* (Cambridge, MA: Perseus Books, 1954). Also see Loris Vezzali and Sofia Stathi, *Intergroup Contact Theory: Recent Developments and Future Directions* (London and New York: Routledge, Taylor & Francis Group, 2016).

so they can feel good enough about each other to work together on the problems that have divided them.

A group called One Small Step is among those taking this approach. Created by StoryCorps, they bring together people across political divides, not so much to discuss their political views—although they do that—but to learn about each other's lived experiences. Through structured conversation, One Small Step helps people move beyond their labels to see each other in their fullness as human beings. "Do we have issues we need to deal with?" one participant asked. "Yes, we do, but we are not going to be able to deal with them if we are yelling and fighting with each other and not listening." Another recounted how "it was important for me to meet someone who didn't have horns and a tail." And yet another mentioned that despite superficial differences in dress and accents, "We're all concerned about our children, about the world we live in," while another regretted that "a lot of people wouldn't even think we should be here talking to each other, but I'm sorry, I disagree."

By creating a genuine connection between strangers across a vast array of groups, they hope to remind people of their common humanity, and in so doing, mend our frayed social fabric one conversation at a time.[201]

In the case of their parent organization, StoryCorps, that is a lot of conversations. Since 2003, StoryCorps has recorded tens of thousands of conversations with over half a million people of all backgrounds and beliefs. Those recordings are now housed at the American Folklife Center at the Library of Congress in Washington, DC, where it comprises the largest digital collection of human voices ever. When StoryCorps surveyed their listeners, 95 percent said the recordings helped them understand the experiences of people different from them. Since 2018, One Small Step has been using that platform to bring people with different political views together to record fifty-minute conversations. Their aim is not to debate their differences but to learn more about one another as people. Their website makes a point of saying that ***anyone anywhere in the United States can sign up to be matched with someone with different political views.*** Founder David Isai hopes enough of us take him up on his offer to realize his dream that Americans consider it their patriotic duty to see the humanity in people with whom they disagree. Wondering what you can do? Sign up and get to know someone outside of your tribe. Then get to know someone else, and then someone else . . . before you know it, strangers may no longer seem so strange.

---

[201] From One Small Step's webpage. For more, go to https://storycorps.org/about/ or see its animated video at https://rb.gy/bjz1rv. If you want to participate, go to https://storycorps.org/discover/onesmallstep/.

Repairing frayed relationships

Resetting the Table (RTT) is a kind of hybrid organization that lies between those taking a more substantive approach and those taking a more relational approach to depolarization.[202] Founded by Rabbi Melissa Weintraub and Eyal Rabinovitch, Resetting the Table cut its teeth on the Israeli–Palestinian conflict, then migrated to the U.S. after the 2016 election surfaced divides that began to look as intractable as those in the Middle East. Concerned by what they saw, they launched a new initiative called Resetting the American Table, aimed at opening up lines of communication and understanding across red-blue-purple divides. They began their work in the U.S. with a listening tour and a series of dialogues in Midwestern counties that swung from Obama to Trump in 2016. Their outreach passed over the usual bridge-building suspects in favor of "the unusual suspects"—dairy farmers, blue-collar workers, Evangelical pastors—ordinary citizens facing the partisan frenzy unfolding across the nation. Since then, they have evolved a multifaceted approach to give citizens, leaders, and communities the support they need to handle even their most charged issues constructively across divides.

I first learned about Resetting the Table in Amanda Ripley's book *High Conflict*, in which Ripley tells the story of RTT's work in 2012 with B'nai Jeshurun, a synagogue known as BJ, located on the Upper West Side in New York City.[203] The rabbis at BJ reached out to RTT for help after they sent an email to their 2,400-member congregation praising the United Nations' vote upgrading Palestine's status. In an internet instant, the email ripped the community apart. Some withheld donations; others left the synagogue. Both were stunned that their rabbis would publicly support an effort they thought threatened Israel's security. The conflict got so bad it ended up on the front page of the *New York Times*.

Though hurt and dismayed, the rabbis apologized, in the hope that it would allow them to move on. But as Ripley notes, "conflict like this doesn't go away. It just goes underground." A year later, it flared back up when BJ's rabbis signed on to a letter criticizing New York City's mayor for pledging loyalty to a pro-Israel lobbying group. Congregants again accused the rabbis of disloyalty to Israel, and even more people left.

Rabbi Matalon considered his options. He could quit, keep his mouth shut, keep on fighting, or do something most of us find terrifically hard to do: lean

---

[202] See Resetting the Table's website at https://www.resettingthetable.org.

[203] My account of the B'nai Jeshurun and the Michigan–New York exchange is based on Amanda Ripley's *High Conflict* and "We Need More 'Good Conflict' in Our Lives. Here's How It Works," *Time*, April 17, 2021.

into conflict and put it to use. He chose to lean in. He wanted to get at the understory behind the conflict and use it to help his congregation break out of the assumptions pushing them into separate camps. For help, he called on fellow rabbi Melissa Weintraub, cofounder of Resetting the Table.

Whenever Weintraub enters a conflict, her first strategy is to listen with genuine curiosity to what's on people's minds and in their hearts. It may sound simple, but as Ripley points out, "almost no one knows how to do it. We jump to conclusions. We think we understand when we don't. We tee up our next point, before the other person has finished talking."

Weintraub's listening helped, a lot. Soon members of the BJ community began listening to one another with the same genuine curiosity evident in Weintraub. They discovered that their conflict was not so much about their particular positions on the Israeli–Palestinian conflict but about the different values and fears surfaced through listening to one another's stories. Even though they still disagreed, their mutual storytelling not only reduced hostility and outrage; it allowed them to see that they all wanted the same thing: "They wanted Israel to be stable and secure and for the Palestinians to have independence and dignity. What they disagreed about—profoundly—was how to get there."[204]

On how to get there, they discovered that there were not just two camps but, like America's tribes, a continuum of views and feelings, many of them complex and mixed because the problem itself was complex and mixed. Their many discoveries over many weeks led to a single conclusion: there is no one easy answer, only complicated, uncertain realities with which they would need to grapple together.

It took time, but through listening to one another's stories and understanding each other's views and fears, they mended the rift that had torn them apart and took up the work of moving forward together as a congregation, committed to Israel's security *and* to Palestinians' independence.

Walking hope into existence

Chinese philosopher Lin Yutang once said that hope is like a road in the country. It comes into existence only after many people walk on it. Tens of thousands of people across our country are walking that hope into existence.[205] In their collective efforts lies a paradoxical truth Václav Havel observed in the 1970s just as

[204] See Ripley, 2021, for the full story on BJ.

[205] To find out about many other organizations tending to our unfinished work, go to https://citizen-connect.us.

the Solidarity movement was gathering strength across the Soviet Bloc: "Perhaps hopelessness is the very soil that nourishes human hope."[206]

I am hoping that more of us join them, that more of us become the finishers to whom President Lincoln referred at Gettysburg when he said: "It is for us the living, rather, to be dedicated here to the unfinished work which they who fought here have thus far so nobly advanced. It is rather for us to be here dedicated to the great task remaining before us—that from these honored dead we take increased devotion to that cause for which they gave the last full measure of devotion—that we here highly resolve that these dead shall not have died in vain—that this nation, under God, shall have a new birth of freedom—and that government of the people, by the people, for the people, shall not perish from the earth."

---

[206] For more on Havel, go to https://www.vhlf.org/havel-in-the-media/living-in-truth/.

NINETEEN

REWRITING
the NEWS
THAT'S FIT
to PRINT

Among the freedoms protected by the Bill of Rights is that of a free press. Our Founders included it to ensure an informed and engaged citizenry, not a polarized and exhausted one. While government has kept its side of the bargain by protecting the press's freedom, the press has not kept its side of the bargain quite as well. In recent and distant years, it has shuttled back and forth between informing, misinforming, and disinforming a public unable to judge which is which.

The result? According to More in Common, people who regularly read the news are almost three times more distorted in their perceptions of their political opponents than those who said they read the news only now and then. "We can't prove that one causes the other," say the researchers, "but these results suggest that rather than making Americans better informed, media coverage is now feeding our misperceptions."[207] This essay looks at how a free press intended to inform the public ended up feeding our misperceptions, then describes what thousands of journalists are doing to transform that trend.

The makings of a downward spiral

Many factors are eating away at the press's ability to keep us well informed and constructively engaged. Among the most obvious are two interrelated trends accelerated by our wallets and clicks: the decline of local news and the rise of

---

[207] "News Media Doesn't Help," More in Common Survey on the Perception Gap, https://perceptiongap.us.

profit-driven national and social media. In a 2021 article, Elaine Godfrey gives an up-close-and-personal account of how the fall of the one and the rise of the other affected her and her hometown fifteen miles west of Burlington, Iowa. The account reads like an obituary written in advance of a death, as it traces the steady decline of her local paper, the *Hawk Eye,* after the national newspaper chain *Gannett* came to town. Godfrey herself reads like a mourner, heartbroken over the disintegrating effects of the paper's decline: "When that tissue disintegrates, something vital rots away. We don't often stop to ponder the way that a newspaper's collapse makes people feel: less connected, more alone. As local news crumbles, so does our tether to one another."[208]

With national news dominating and dividing our attention, citizens are pretty evenly split on whether today's press helps democracy, hurts democracy, or neither helps nor hurts democracy.[209] But as Allen Arthur of Solutions Journalism Network points out, ". . . slams on 'the media' as a monolith miss some pretty important things . . . Underneath 'the media' there are many journalists just as discontented with 'the way it's always been done' as anyone."[210]

And that brings us to an equally harmful but less obvious factor undercutting the press's ability to keep us well informed and engaged: the way journalism has always been done. "If forced to spell out their theory of change, journalists will often describe an outrage model," says journalism professor Jay Rosen. "It goes like this: Investigative reporting reveals incompetence, corruption, poor leadership or bad decision-making. The outrage that results gets the attention of people in power. If the public demands change, and the political system sticks with it long enough, the newspaper will report on those things too, and eventually there will be change." Trouble is, while anger can expose a problem, says Rosen, it cannot by itself uncover solutions. It can only fill the public square with the fear, outrage, and blame.[211]

In the 1980s, political consultant Roger Ailes exploited the outrage model to get his clients Ronald Reagan and George H.W. Bush elected presidents, devising what he called the "orchestra pit theory of politics." As he explained to reporter Judy Woodruff:[212]

[208] Elaine Godfrey, "What We Lost When Gannett Came to Town," *Atlantic*, October 5, 2021.

[209] "Americans and the News Media: What they do—and don't—understand about each other," the Media Insight Project, June 2018.

[210] Allen Arthur, *The Response*, Solutions Journalism Network, December 2022, https://rb.gy/07rykh.

[211] Cf. David Bornstein told Jay Rosen. See Jay Rosen, "What Does Constructive Journalism Construct?" Keynote speech to the Bonn Institute, April 27, 2022.

[212] Tim Dickinson, "Roger Ailes' Keys to Campaign Success: 'Mistakes, Pictures and Attacks,'" *Rolling Stone*, June 6, 2011.

Roger Ailes: Let's face it, there are three things that the media are interested in: pictures, mistakes and attacks. That's the one sure way of getting coverage. . . . It's my orchestra pit theory of politics. You have two guys on stage and one guy says, "I have a solution to the Middle East problem," and the other guy falls in the orchestra pit, who do you think is going to be on the evening news?

Judy Woodruff: So you're saying the notion of the candidate saying, "I want to run for President because I want to do something for this country," is crazy.

Roger Ailes: Suicide.

Ever since Ailes and long before, political operatives and candidates have been playing the "independent" press for chumps. You can see it most clearly today in the over-coverage of extremists in the House who routinely throw themselves into orchestra pits for attention's sake. In 2017, journalism professors Michael Wagner and Mike Gruszczynski found that ideologically extreme members in the House are covered more than those with more moderate positions. The implication for us?

If journalists are systematically more likely to choose to cover those who speak the most stridently on the Congressional floor, they are likely to quote ideological extremists who tend to speak in intense, partisan terms (Morris, 2001). This is important because, as Druckman, Peterson, and Slothuus (2013) have shown, individuals respond to competing frames by preferring to endorse the argument coming from the person's favored political party when the media present a polarized political environment, while the same arguments, in a moderate political environment, nudge people to favor the stronger argument, regardless of the argument's source.[213]

The news business is the classic siloed system in which one group (news media) is responsible for doing one thing (identifying problems) while another group (the government and/or the public) is responsible for doing another (solving problems), with no integration across boundaries and no responsibility on anyone's part for the societal results they together produce.

Redefining what news is fit to print

Today a growing national movement is afoot to create a new kind of journalism. Within this movement are thousands of journalists who bring a wider lens to the

[213] Michael W. Wagner and Mike Gruszczynski, "Who Gets Covered? Ideological Extremity and News Coverage of Members of the U.S. Congress, 1993 to 2013," *Journalism & Mass Communication Quarterly*, vol. 95, no. 3 (2017): 1–21.

problems they cover, who dig deeper into the "understory" behind conflicts, and who unearth insights and solutions that inform, surprise, and engage the reader. These journalists are rebuilding trust with communities by helping them solve their stickiest problems, in one case uncovering successful efforts to end homelessness in a city, a county, and a country, something many have said is impossible.[214] The journalists investigating and writing these stories subscribe to what Jay Rosen once said: "somewhere around the globe, good people have solved a problem that other people, living on the same planet, still need to solve."[215] And they are gaining traction, helping journalists in newsrooms around the globe reframe their role and redefine their craft, so they can uncover new solutions and distribute them more widely for more and more of us to see and use.

> **More than 600 news organizations and 30,000 journalists to date have already taken part in solutions journalism training or published solution-oriented stories.[216]**

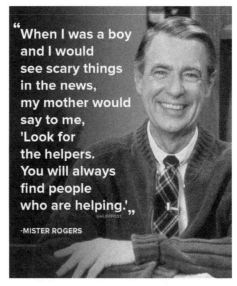

Among those at the forefront of this movement is Solutions Journalism Network (SJN). Founded in 2013 by David Bornstein, Courtney E. Martin, and Tina Rosenberg, the folks at SJN work tirelessly with news organizations around the world to build a global network of newsrooms and journalists who use solutions journalism, not just to inform the public but to strengthen communities, increase civic engagement, and improve public discourse.[217] Perhaps most important given today's rampant mistrust of government and electoral politics, they are

---

[214] Allen Arthur, *The Response,* Solutions Journalism Network, https://rb.gy/8t83n.

[215] Rosen, "What Does Constructive Journalism Construct?"

[216] Solutions Journalism website: https://www.solutionsjournalism.org/impact; https://learninglab.solutionsjournalism.org.

[217] Ibid.

helping journalists in hundreds of newsrooms cover our elections, government, politics, and democracy more constructively.

Over the past ten years, their combined efforts have begun to redefine the kind of news that is fit to print. Instead of dividing the world into right and wrong, their stories uncover the moral ambiguities we need to understand to better address complex people and problems. Instead of simplifying narratives, they complicate them to get at the hidden truth simplified narratives miss. Instead of reporting point-counterpoint accusations, their stories are based on verifiable facts and provide useful context. Instead of instilling a sense of helplessness, they cultivate a sense of efficacy by focusing on the helpers, not just the harmers. And instead of blaming one or another person or party for problems, they investigate and uncover the root causes behind problems and the creative solutions people are inventing to address them.

Another group of journalists called Images and Voices of Hope (IVOH) is following a similar path. They take tragic stories of natural and manmade disasters—from tornados and hurricanes to shootings and bombings—and turn them into stories of recovery, restoration, and resilience. They go beyond the immediacy of a disaster to examine its longer-term effects, and they stay long enough to recount how people and communities pick up the pieces of their lives and make something good out of them.[218] These "restorative narratives," as they call them, do not limit their focus to the hardships people face, although they cover those too. They focus on what people make of those hardships and how they rise above whatever upended their lives.[219]

All of us know from experience that consuming news can be stressful, sometimes very stressful. According to a Harvard Public Health study, stressed-out people cite news as their third biggest stressor out of ten. The second is hearing about what our government and politicians are doing. Given much of that comes from the news, that makes news doubly stressful.[220] Those looking to reinvent the news attribute the stress to journalists' unrelenting tendency to focus on the worst events of the day. As the saying goes, "If it bleeds, it leads." That "what-bleeds-leads" practice skews reality so much that we rarely see anything that anyone is doing to stem the bleeding and make things better.

[218] For more on restorative narrative, go to Images and Voices of Hope, https://rb.gy/h5uut.

[219] For an excellent example of restorative narrative, see *Restoring the World*, showcased in Essay 16: "Putting Faith in Friendship."

[220] The Burden of Stress in America, https://media.npr.org/documents/2014/july/npr_rwjf_harvard_stress_poll.pdf.

That is a big problem, because we rely on the news to see what is *really* going on. That means the news, quite literally, stands between us and reality, filtering what we see and do not see and how we see it. That filter's built-in negative bias is making more and more of us feel so helpless that we are acting more and more helpless. I suspect the 87 percent that More in Common calls the exhausted majority might more aptly be called the helpless majority, made all but invisible by the 13 percent on the far left and right getting 87 percent of the attention.

Journalist Natasha Peters at Images and Voices of Hope (IVOH) wants to turn that sense of helplessness into helpfulness by changing the way news filters reality. She wants to create a more accurate picture of the world, not by excluding negative news but by including positive news. "Research has found that uplifting news can motivate people to do good in the world," says Peters. She goes on to say that a 2011 study in the *Journal of Personality and Social Psychology* looked at the "warm, uplifting feeling people get from watching someone act with compassion or courage—a feeling that psychologists refer to as 'moral elevation.' This feeling of elevation supports people's belief in the goodness of humanity, induces positive emotions, and inspires people to act more altruistically."[221] Research shows that most readers are hungry for news that elevates rather than enervates them.[222] That is likely why more and more journalists at mainstream outlets are making resilience and recovery a part of their work, among them *Los Angeles Times* reporter Anh Do, *New York Times* reporter Andrea Elliot, and *San Francisco Chronicle* reporter Kevin Fagan.

Still, in case you are tempted to dismiss these innovations as feel-good, left-leaning blips, consider the *Dispatch*. Cofounders Stephen F. Hayes, Jonah Goldberg, and Toby Stock are neither solutions journalists nor in the business of publishing restorative narratives. They took a different tack to reinventing the news. They launched the *Dispatch* in 2018 to undercut the growing alliance between right-wing media and the Republican Party. It is now one of the most popular subscription-based, ad-free magazines online, giving readers factually grounded journalism from a conservative perspective. In one email, they promise to slow "the news-cycle down a bit to provide context and perspective . . . without the noise and clutter so frustrating to those of us who just want to stay informed. So, no pop-ups, no

---

[221] Natasha Peters, "Restorative Narratives: Defining a New Strength-Based Genre," April 13, 2023, https://rb.gy/h5uut; Karl Aquino, Brent McFerran, and Marjorie Laven, "Moral Identity and the Experience of Moral Elevation in Response to Acts of Uncommon Goodness," *Journal of Personality and Social Psychology*, vol. 100, no. 4 (2011): 703–718.

[222] Corinne Sanders, "6 Research-Backed Reasons Why Reading Positive News Is Good For You," https://rb.gy/wiak2.

auto-play videos, no clickbait ad boxes, no random sound suddenly blaring from your device." In taking this stand, they have two aims: keeping their readers well informed "without losing their minds" *and* redefining the business of journalism. "With every new member of *The Dispatch,*" one email reads, "we send a powerful message that good journalism can be a good business. And if good journalism is a good business, we'll have more people doing good journalism."

The founders of the *Dispatch* are not the only conservatives to turn to online subscriptions as an alternative to mainstream online media. In December 2018, Republican political strategist Sarah Longwell and political commentators Bill Kristol and Charlie Sykes launched the *Bulwark,* a subscription-based newsletter and website delivering an unvarnished, smart, and thoughtful take on our political reality since the 2016 election of Trump. All three are "Never-Trumpers," neoconservatives whose news and opinions draw our attention to the popular and institutional forces that brought Trump to power and may again. Their editor, J.V. Last, writes a column that distills current events and commentaries, leavened by movie clips and GIFs, to raise fundamental questions about who we are and who we want to be as a people. "The People are the Problem," reads the headline to a column reciting all the choices We the People have made to get us where we are today. Unlike so much of mainstream media, J.V. Last and all the others at the *Bulwark* prompt us to think more deeply about where we are and where we want to go.

Reinventing the media business

In 2017, three friends—Chris Best, Hamish McKenzie, and Jairaj Sethi—launched Substack, a subscription-based email news service through which the *Dispatch* and the *Bulwark* were both launched. All three were fed up with online media's pop-ups, clickbait ad boxes, and algorithms designed to keep people amped up and hooked. They wanted to create an alternative business model that connects writers directly with readers and builds long-term relationships with both.

Today Substack has over 500,000 dedicated paying subscribers, its readers count in the millions, and its top ten authors collectively make over $20 million per year.[223] According to search engine expert Brian Dean, demand for non-ad-based media models is taking off with newsletters leading the pack.[224] Other platforms

---

[223] Brian Dean, "Substack User and Revenue Statistics (2023)," https://rb.gy/4iuvb. Also see Baidhurya Mani, "30+ Top Substack Statistics 2023," https://rb.gy/lgtpz.

[224] Dean, "Substack User and Revenue Statistics (2023)."

are now rushing into the space to meet those needs. Today platforms like Ghost, beehiiv, and others all offer writers a way to monetize their writing and get their message to readers.

The competition was timely. As 2023 drew to a close, Substack came under intense scrutiny for publishing people and content that even Facebook and pre-Musk Twitter banned for spreading misinformation or hate. Substack founder Hamish McKenzie bristled at the comparison. "Facebook and Twitter and others who are taking a harder-line approach to content moderation are more obliged to, because they're amplification machines," said McKenzie. "They are giving you news feeds that are sorted by content that is highly engaging. It encourages the production of this divisive content. These are the world's most powerful machines ever to encourage the spread of disinformation, and so the burden of action on them is higher."[225] Maybe so, but given that our public discourse is increasingly riddled with hate and our public square with mass murders, you would think any burden of action would be worth bearing.

One of Substack's most vocal critics, long-term Substacker Jonathan Katz, shares that view. In November 2023, Katz published an article in the *Atlantic* cataloguing the result of Substack's lax approach. "An informal search of the Substack website and of extremist Telegram channels that circulate Substack posts turns up scores of white-supremacist, neo-Confederate, and explicitly Nazi newsletters on Substack," writes Katz. Most of these online sites spread conspiracy theories and misinformation known to fuel violence, including mass murders.[226]

So what are Substackers like Jonathan Katz to do? For now, he is staying. "Every platform and publication I've written for—including, with respect, the *Atlantic*—has done many things with which I strongly disagree and don't like associating myself," Katz told his readers. "Also, I was here before the Nazis, and I think they should leave, not me." Whether they leave depends not only on business owners like McKenzie, but on the incentives we create for them, as citizens and journalists.

[225] See Joe Pompeo, "'There Has to Be a Line:' Substack's Founders Dive Headfirst Into the Culture Wars," *Vanity Fair,* May 23, 2022; Benjamin Mullin and Katie Robertson, "Are We Past Peak Newsletter?" *New York Times,* October 23, 2022; Anna Wiener, "Is Substack the Media Future We Want?" *New Yorker,* December 28, 2020; and Spencer Bokat-Lindell, "Is the Rise of the Substack Economy Bad for Democracy?" *New York Times,* July 2, 2021.

[226] Rachel Hatzipanagos, "How online hate turns into real-life violence," *New York Times*, November 30, 2018

Which future do we, as citizens and as journalists, want?

Whether or not these new-form journalists, media outlets, or news platforms think of themselves as reinventing journalism or the news business more broadly, they are all promoting a new and increasingly successful way of informing and engaging the public. Together they are proof points that money can be made by inviting citizens to use their frontal lobes to think, instead of sucking them down into their brain stems to quiver in fear or hate. They are the classic disruptors in an industry overdue for disruption.

Looking to the future, Amanda Ripley believes more and more online news sites will struggle to make ends meet with clickbait headlines and ad revenue, and that more and more outlets will turn to subscribers to finance their reporting. "That means they have to shift from a one-night-stand business model to a long-term relationship with readers—which has to be based on something deeper than cats and Trump tweets," says Ripley.[227]

In 2017, journalist Tom Junod wrote an article for *Esquire* on Fred Rogers, host of the children's educational TV program *Mister Rogers' Neighborhood*. The two eventually became friends, and their friendship eventually became a film called *A Beautiful Day in the Neighborhood* starring Tom Hanks as Rogers. After the film's release, its screenwriters shared with Junod the contents of a file Rogers kept on their friendship. In the folder was a note written by Rogers:

Journalists are human beings not automatons. Human beings not stenographers.

Journalists have a duty to let their outrage show through when they come across injustice.

Journalists need to let their compassion show through for other people's suffering.

Journalists need to let their ahhh (wonder) show through when they witness the glory of life . . . they have as much responsibility to celebrate life and the good-ness of it as they do to root out evil.

The same holds true for us as consumers of the news. Like journalists, we can at times feel torn between stories that capture our amygdalae, fuel our anxiety, and evoke our anger, and those that capture a sense of wonder, fuel empathy, and

---

[227] Amanda Ripley, "Complicating the Narratives: What if journalists covered controversial issues differently—based on how humans actually behave when they are polarized and suspicious?" Solutions Journalism, January 11, 2019, https://rb.gy/3shbr.

deepen understanding. As journalists and as citizens in our democracy, we have the right to choose which to put at the center of our lives.

It is a choice reminiscent of the old Cherokee story about two wolves.[228] One is full of anger, envy, greed, arrogance, resentment, lies, false pride, superiority, and ego. The other is full of empathy, generosity, truth, compassion, love, hope, humility, and kindness.

The one that grows is the one we feed.

---

[228] The origins of this story are contested. Whatever its origins, its moral is clear. For a video of the story, go to https://www.youtube.com/watch?v=x95_BTeanI8.

TWENTY

OUTWITTING MISINFORMATION[229]

On July 20, 2023, just as the 2024 campaign was ramping up, the *Dispatch* reported, "Earlier this week, a Ron DeSantis-aligned super PAC released a 30-second ad in Iowa detailing former President Donald Trump's spat with the state's popular Republican governor, Kim Reynolds. 'I endorsed her, did big rallies, and when she won, now she wants to remain 'neutral,' Trump says before a narrator asks why he's fighting with his fellow Republicans. It's a fair hit—several GOP strategists in Iowa think it will cost Trump—but there's just one problem with the ad. Trump never said those words."[230]

The DeSantis super PAC, Never Back Down, "said" them. The PAC created a fake yet true-to-Trump sounding audio of Trump reading the statement aloud. And that's not all. The report goes on: "Last month, the DeSantis campaign released a video going after Trump for his refusal to fire Dr. Anthony Fauci during the pandemic—and the spot included a fake, AI-generated image of the former president hugging the famous immunologist."[231]

Trump, of course, is not the only target, as the *Dispatch* recounts: "When President Joe Biden announced his reelection campaign in April, the Republican National Committee released an AI-generated video depicting several apocalyptic-looking scenes and warning another Biden term would make them a reality. And lest you think this is a purely Republican phenomenon, an audio deepfake released the day before the Chicago mayoral election earlier this year portrayed the less progressive Democratic candidate in the Chicago Mayoral election as condoning police brutality."[232]

---

[229] This essay was co-written with Andrew Doty of the Rebuild Congress Initiative.

[230] Declan Garvey, Esther Eaton, Mary Trimble, Grayson Logue, and Jacob Wendler, "AI Infiltrates the 2024 Race," *Dispatch*, July 20, 2023. https://rb.gy/rok3a.

[231] Ibid.

[232] Ibid.

> **As if fake facts and cockamamie conspiracy theories were not bad enough, now we have AI generated images and recordings virtually impossible to distinguish from the real thing.**

What is an already frazzled citizenry to do? How can we tell what is fake and what is fact? What can we do to protect ourselves from those treating us like chumps?

So far, misinformation and disinformation are winning today's information war

We have more access to more information from more sources today than ever before: radio, TV, online news, blogs, social media, anti-social media, twenty-four-hour cable news. That feeling of "viral vertigo" we get trying to make sense of it all is spreading out of control through an "infodemic" in which false or misleading rumors and hoaxes circulate at lightning speed through already-scared populations.[233] When COVID-19 circled the globe in 2020, it spawned an especially virulent infodemic of unproven remedies and conspiracy theories, encouraging people to try untested treatments and discount public health advice.

Figure 20.1: Misinformation and Disinformation

- **Misinformation** is false or inaccurate information: getting the facts wrong.

- **Disinformation** is false information deliberately intended to mislead: intentionally misstating the facts.

- **The spread of misinformation and disinformation affects our ability** to improve public health, address climate change, maintain a stable democracy.

- **By providing valuable insight** into why we are likely to believe mis-inform-mation and disinformation, psychological science can help us protect ourselves against its ill effects.[234]

[233] See Claire Wardle's YouTube training video on infodemics, "Why misinformation matters," https://rb.gy/phoii.

[234] "Misinformation and Disinformation," *American Psychological Association*, https://rb.gy/wwcaf. Edited for brevity.

This not only harmed the health of thousands of individuals; it undercut efforts to fight the pandemic, fueling its spread. Over time, infodemics like the one accompanying COVID-19 cause truth and trust to suffer, as people struggle to separate truth from falsehood and expert from quack—all of it weakening our ability as a society to create the shared reality needed to address shared challenges.

Inoculating against misinformation and disinformation

In a TEDx talk titled "How to Be an Ally for Truth," Eric Schurenberg, the former CEO of Mansueto Ventures, gives three pieces of advice on how to protect truth when the click of a button or the tap of a screen can send a deadly falsehood around the globe faster than COVID-19. [235] The first is to be wary of any claim that is so abstract or fanciful it cannot be disproven, especially if it conforms to our preconceived notions. Trust only claims tested with verifiable facts. The second is to test any claims sent to you against verifiable facts before sending them on to others. If you cannot find any facts to support the claim, ditch in the trash. The third is to be on the lookout for cognitive biases that make it hard to suss out the truth. Acquaint yourself with the many biases that cloud our judgment, and think about your thinking before infecting others with it. [236] Be especially hyper-vigilant when it comes to the most deadly and common bias of all: confirmation bias, the tendency to look only for information that confirms our beliefs while ignoring any information that disconfirms them.

To illustrate how ingrained and out of our awareness this bias operates, a community educator on YouTube conducted an informal experiment in a park full of people. [237] He asked willing passersby to guess the rule behind a sequence of three numbers he presented: 2, 4, and 8. To make it easier, he told them that they could propose their own sequences of numbers to test if those too followed the rule. Despite repeatedly guessing sequences they thought conformed to the hidden rule, no one got any closer to correctly predicting what the rule was *until they proposed sequences that broke the rule.* Only then did they finally land on the answer.

It takes only one exception to discover that reality is not as simple as our preconceived beliefs lead us to think. But you cannot discover that exception unless you look for it.

---

[235] See Eric Schurenberg's TEDx talk at https://rb.gy/1c33p.

[236] For an extensive list of cognitive biases, see "Cognitive Biases: A list of the most relevant biases in behavioral economics," by The Decision Lab. https://rb.gy/vxfmm.

[237] To find out what the rule is (but only after you guess!), see the video at https://rb.gy/e76f1.

Debunking is too late; we need to "prebunk"

Researchers in a number of leading universities are helping us fight infodemics on a large scale by educating people to recognize and counter misinformation and disinformation *before* it takes hold. Through an approach they call "prebunking," they focus on manipulative tactics and narratives rather than specific claims. In the web-based game Bad News, for example, they ask game participants to assume the role of those creating fake news to increase their awareness of six prevalent misinformation techniques. Rigorous testing of the game with German, Greek, Polish, and Swedish players revealed substantial decreases in the trustworthiness of manipulative information.[238]

Educational psychologist Dr. Doug Lombardi at the University of Maryland's Science Learning Research Group takes a similar approach. In September 2022, he and his group collaborated with a few other institutions to launch a four-year science education initiative.[239] That initiative, which involved around a hundred teachers and a thousand students in middle and high schools in Philadelphia and Georgia, introduced students to a critical assessment technique known as "lateral reading," helping students assess authors' credibility, a source's reliability, and scientific validity by examining materials concurrently.

Are conspiracy theories a problem of belief or belonging?

"We have to consider that conspiracy theorists are not just joining these groups for no reason," says Peter McIndoe after launching a fake conspiracy theory movement to better understand conspiracy theories and those spreading them. "They're getting rewards that we are all looking for: a sense of purpose and community." In a TED talk that went viral, Peter describes how he played a conspiracy theorist for four years, traveling around the country and organizing protests to spread the word: Birds are not real; they are mechanical spies—or, in the words of the movement's slogan, "If it flies, it spies." His experience taught him, and it now teaches us, to remember that human beings live behind all those theories swirling around us.

---

[238] Jon Roozenbeek, Sander van der Linden, and Thomas Nygren, "Prebunking interventions based on 'inoculation' theory can reduce susceptibility to misinformation across cultures," *HKS Misinformation Review*, https://doi.org/10.37016//mr-2020-008.

[239] Tori DeAngelis, "Psychologists are taking aim at misinformation with these powerful strategies," *Monitor on Psychology*, vol. 54, no. 1 (2023): 44, https://www.apa.org/monitor/2023/01/trends-taking-aim-misinformation.

Calling for a new solution to a new problem, he asks a fundamental question: *"What if, by addressing belief before belonging, we're starting the conversation in the wrong place?"*[240]

Instead of judging "crazies" for believing this or that theory, he says, perhaps we should look "under the hood" at what makes people vulnerable to conspiracy theories. He encourages us to see those with "bewildering" beliefs as "fellow human beings who want to believe in something, who want to belong, just like all of us in this room." During his four-year charade, he found that arguing over beliefs got people nowhere. Even though he was not in reality a conspiracy theorist, he still felt hurt and angry when people dismissed him as "crazy" or "stupid" for believing birds were not real. He realized that if *he* could feel so defensive that he wanted to cling more tightly to *fake* beliefs, those actually holding such beliefs would do the same, if not worse, concluding, "We're going to end up with more echo chambers, more disinformation and more polarization." The alternative?

> **"Let's direct our energy toward the crisis of belonging. And then maybe we will understand the crisis of belief."**

This is no silver-bullet remedy. It takes hard work to ensure that those around us feel a sense of belonging. Then again, knocking down one belief after another is like playing Whac-A-Mole. You hit one theory here, only to find another popping up there. In the long run, addressing the crisis of belonging infecting our society will bring us closer to the shared reality that would make all our lives easier.

In the short run, we can get by cultivating greater awareness of our cognitive biases and by deploying prebunking techniques. We can also revise our laws to address advances in technology, as illustrated below. But there is no getting around the deep-seated human need to belong. If that need is not met one way, it will be met in another. Best we help people meet it in ways that serve rather than harm us and our society.

Bringing laws into the twenty-first century

Professor Mary Anne Franks, President and Legislative & Tech Policy Director of the Cyber Civil Rights Initiative, wants to update our laws so we can better

---

[240] Peter McIndoe's TED Talk, "Birds aren't real? How a conspiracy theory takes flight," https://rb.gy/m8kls. Also, see Taylor Lorenz, "Birds Aren't Real, or Are They? Inside a Gen Z Conspiracy Theory," *New York Times,* December 9, 2021, https://rb.gy/1phtm.

combat misinformation. Following her success at advocating for laws against what is called "revenge porn," Professor Franks is now combatting the creation and distribution of imagery manipulated to appear authentic when it really is not. In popular parlance, these images and videos are often known as "deepfakes," but Franks wants to call them what they are: digital forgeries.

Franks recommends criminalizing unlabeled digital forgeries so that social media companies can be held accountable for digital forgeries disseminated on their platforms. In case you think this would be unfair to social media companies, consider that in every context other than the tech industry and the firearms industry, contributory responsibility is always a factor in liability law. If, for example, you have a hotel that doesn't provide adequate security measures to prevent a gunman from bringing twenty-two suitcases full of weapons up to his room over the course of a few days, enabling him to commit the deadliest mass shooting in U.S. history, you may be liable. MGM recently agreed to pay $800M to shooting victims to settle just such a lawsuit arising from the shooting at the Mandalay Bay Hotel, even though MGM did not kill anyone.[241]

Franks argues that online businesses ought to assume the same kind of responsibility and liability for contributing to criminal activity as brick-and-mortar offline businesses like MGM must assume under the law.[242] Earlier this year, legislation proposed by Professor Franks was introduced to Congress. Called SAFE TECH (Safeguarding Against Fraud, Exploitation, Threats, Extremism and Consumer Harms), the legislation would update the law so that social media companies could be held accountable for how their platforms are used, including for cyberstalking, online harassment, and discrimination.

Meanwhile, what can you do? You can guard against your own cognitive biases, understand how manipulative strategies manipulate, look for data that disconfirm claims, support legislation like SAFE TECH, and foster a sense of belonging in people wherever and whenever you can. But above all else:

Practice safe text: do your research before you text or click that "share" button.

---

[241] "Court approves $800M settlement for MGM Resorts, Vegas shooting victims," September 30, 2020. https://rb.gy/3n7ts.

[242] Argument advanced by Prof. Franks at the University of Notre Dame panel, "Deepfake Conference Panel III: Marginalized Populations," https://rb.gy/v2c41.

TWENTY-ONE

HELPING

from

THE PERIPHERY

The culture wars that are driving us crazy are not going away any time soon. They are what political journalist Jane Coaston calls "forever wars"—wars no one can win because the battleground is always shifting, as is the way people keep score. Meanwhile, casualties mount: "Every decision, even decisions that have nothing to do with culture, even decisions that seem completely untethered to the culture war, become part of the culture war."[243] Once a decision or an issue gets tossed into the fight, facts are the first to go. So quickly are facts evaporating from our political landscape that it is fast becoming an empirical desert. Yet we keep sacrificing facts—or worse, inventing them—to win an unwinnable war over whose values should prevail. Why do we keep doing it? Why do we keep sending our most sacred values into ungodly wars no one can win? Among many possible reasons, three stand out:

- The values we hold, as a people and as a nation, conflict with one another.

- We cannot fact-find our way out of conflicts that revolve around values.

- Our win-lose approach to conflict prevents us from inventing a new way out together.

Today our toughest political conflicts all get adjudicated sooner or later in the court of values, where facts do not play a determinative role. Problem is, while we have become quite adept at dealing with facts, *even* those that conflict,

---

[243] "How the Culture Wars Weren't Won (with Jane Coaston)," on Sarah Longwell's *The Focus Group*, a Bulwark podcast. March 18, 2023.

we remain relatively clueless as a society in dealing with values, *especially* those that conflict.

And for good reason. Who is to say one value is better or more important than another? On what basis do you determine that, especially in a world that has all but abandoned facts? It is the single biggest conundrum we face as a pluralist democracy built on a multiplicity of values. Until we make progress on that conundrum, we cannot construct a moral foundation upon which we can all stand without tearing one another down. In the meantime, extremists on the far left and right will continue to take a jackhammer to that foundation, threatening its structural integrity and putting us, our future, and our democracy at risk.

> **Those of us within the quieter majority, pushed to the periphery by louder voices on the far left and right, are in the best position to help by doing two things this essay illustrates:**

- Resist the temptation to join one or another polarized side *or* to sit on the sidelines.

- Help those in the value conflict come closer together, so they don't drift further apart.

Focus on winning the peace, not a lose-lose war

The deadliest battle fought during the Civil War took place at Antietam on September 17, 1862, where, by the end of the day, 12,401 Union soldiers and 10,316 Confederate soldiers were dead, wounded, or missing. Because no clear winner or loser emerged from the carnage, most historical accounts use the word "inconclusive" to describe the battle's outcome, saying it was "a draw." What a curiously sad accounting. You would think loss of life so monumental, suffered on both sides, would suggest one conclusive outcome: *two losers, no winners.* But that is not how we are brought up to think in our win-lose culture, so we end up calling lose-lose outcomes like this "a draw."[244]

Today some of our costliest lose-lose battles are taking place in school board meetings on the same cultural grounds fought during the Civil War. On this contested ground, parents and educators frequently face off against one another over what curriculum to teach (or cancel) and what books to read (or cancel). These

---

[244] See "Antietam: Sharpsburg," American Battlefield Trust, https://rb.gy/zkjf.

Antietam 2016 | Photo by D.M. Smith

fraught battles make clear that while the North won the Civil War, our nation has yet to win the peace. Rabbi Jonathan Sacks' distinction between our *social contract* as a nation and our *social covenant* as a people helps explain why. While a social contract addresses positional power within a legal political framework, a social covenant speaks to the informal values that shape how we live together in a pluralist society. A social covenant relies on moral commitments, not coercion; on shared values and ideals, not law and punishment; on inspiration, not obligation, as a means for pursuing the common good.[245] Both are necessary, but as Seth Kaplan, an expert in fragile states, points out: "A society that has reached agreement on its fundamental principles and values . . . through a social covenant is much better equipped to forge a sustainable social contract than one divided by stark fault lines."[246]

Commentator David French makes an observation that goes a long way toward explaining why we have yet to forge such a covenant:

> We're caught in a vicious cycle. Radicals tend to alienate the majority—*causing them to retreat from politics*. After all, who needs that level of anger in their lives? At the same time, radicals tend to radicalize their targets and further radicalize each other. And because radicals are more energized and engaged than anybody else, they can't help but exercise disproportionate influence in shaping our perceptions of the other side.[247]

[245] Jonathan Sacks, *The Home We Build Together: Recreating Society* (New York: Continuum, 2007).

[246] Seth Kaplan, "Social covenants and social contracts in transition," Norwegian Peacebuilding Resource Centre, February 2014.

[247] David French, "Activism and Apathy Are Poisoning American Politics," *Dispatch,* January 1, 2023, https://rb.gy/mhygh. My emphasis.

> **To disrupt this cycle, those of us pushed to the periphery must stop retreating. We must stand our ground, and we must do so without shouting or name-calling or belittling *anyone*.**

That is what the folks in Billings, Montana, did when White neighbors escorted Black neighbors to their church after skinheads sought to intimidate its congregants. It is also what happened when citizens across Billings hung paper menorahs in their windows after an antisemitic group threw a rock through the window of a six-year-old boy's room, shattering the menorah he had put in his window for Hanukkah. These actions, taken by people like you and me, inspired the Not In Our Town (NIOT) movement.[248] As Essay 10 illustrates, that movement now helps citizens across the country take a stand every day for values most of us hold dear.

"We simply cannot delegate our political and cultural engagement to the angriest wings of American life," says David French. "They'll drive us apart even when our differences are not that stark."[249] As individuals, we may feel helpless and exhausted, but if we stand together, we can create more power than those forces dividing us.

Create common ground for the common good

In his last book, Jonathan Sacks wrote that the moral challenge of divided times is to restore the common good by competing less and cooperating more. He understood that this would not be easy. Competition and cooperation call on two very different instincts, one for aggression, the other for altruism.[250] But as Sacks saw it, we must nevertheless try. This is especially true for those among us who are perched on the periphery of conflict.

> **Those on the periphery of a conflict can see and do things that those caught up in the conflict cannot.**

To see what I mean, imagine a school board meeting of the kind we witness almost daily, complete with activist parents coming out in full force to yell at

---

[248] See Essay 9: "Taking a Stand."

[249] French, "Activism and Apathy."

[250] Jonathan Sacks, *Morality: Restoring the Common Good in Divided Times* (London: Hodder & Stoughton, 2020), 252–253.

each other and at the educators and school board members many consider their enemy. Now imagine that a few concerned citizens, fed up with this nonstop rancor sidelining their children's education, decide to activate a phone tree before one of those meetings, calling on their friends to help.

When they arrive early for the meeting, they feel alert and engaged, as they quietly occupy the periphery of the room, standing one or two rows deep. Shortly afterward, a steady stream of parents takes their appointed seats in folding chairs laid out in rows facing a large black table behind which members of the education board sit. Those sitting in rows and those behind the table speak among themselves as the clock ticks down to the scheduled time for the meeting to begin. Those on the periphery remain quiet.

Just as the chair calls the meeting to order, one of the parents interrupts her. "You have no right to impose this curriculum on our kids!" she yells at them. "It is corrupting our children, and we demand that you vote it down tonight!" Others join in and a cacophony of angry voices fills the room, as conflicting placards telling the board what to do stab at the air. At first, the board chair struggles desperately to regain control—shouting into the din, pounding the table with her gavel—but when she realizes she is hopelessly outnumbered and outshouted, she gives up, pushing her chair back, wrapping her arms across her chest.

Then something happens that has never happened before. An ever so quiet shushing sound coming from the parents on the periphery slowly fills the room. It is the kind of sound parents use, not to silence but to calm a distraught child, as if to say, "Shh. It's okay. Shh. You're okay." At first, the sound is almost imperceptible amidst the fracas, but as it continues to waft across the room, those yelling take notice. Disconcerted by the unexpected sound, the yelling slowly ceases. They have no idea why these people on the periphery are shushing quietly in unison. When one of them finally asks, three people on the periphery hold up a ten-foot-long placard that reads: "Let's stop yelling and start talking. For our kids' sakes."

Might this or some other out-of-the-box passive disruption make a difference? Psychological research on self-control suggests it might. When people get caught up in hot conflicts—and all value conflicts are hot conflicts—their brain's hot system takes over, and they lose the ability to think constructively or to see how their actions might be making things worse, not just for others but for themselves.[251] Those of us on the periphery of a hot conflict can see things those in the

---

[251] See Essay 6: "Conflict for Better and for Worse: When conflicts grow hot, our hot systems kick in."

midst of action cannot. That peripheral vision allows us to spot things we can use to interrupt the hot system's grip, to force those caught up in the conflict to go off script, slowing them down and giving them pause.

In that pause, someone on the periphery suggests that the large group break into small groups to share without interruption their concerns and ideas. To keep the momentum going, a few folks on the periphery quietly and calmly start moving chairs into smaller circles. Someone else suggests that the groups include people with different viewpoints and that they report out to the larger group afterward on what they discover. A few of the less polarized people in the still-somewhat-stupefied larger group follow their move, leading others to join them, dividing into twelve smaller groups. Later, after each group reports out its findings, someone else on the periphery suggests that the board continue this type of deliberation until they together come up with a plan the whole community can live with, not just one or another group. She then recommends they consider using the "one-text procedure," which uses different views and values to invent options no one group could imagine on its own.[252] Despite a few bumps along the way, the meeting ends with people who have rarely spoke with one another walking out into the night together.

Sound far-fetched?

By at least one account, it is not far-fetched. In "Stopping culture wars in their tracks," journalist Courtney Martin recounts how Middletown, Ohio, derailed culture wars over masks and school curricula that were disrupting their kids' education. The story starts shortly after Middletown's first Black school superintendent, Marlon Styles, took office.[253] Mr. Styles came to the job with high hopes. He wanted to "electrify the culture" and involve the community in the workings of the school district. He inspired his four hundred employees to launch a campaign called #MiddieRising as a rallying cry for the whole city. "T-shirts were made, banners were hung, videos were produced showing students', parents', and teachers' Middie pride." He recruited volunteers to form a committee to hear quarterly briefings and to spread the word on what the district was doing to serve kids. Though called the Key Communicators, in Styles' mind, they were always "the positive gossipers."

---

[252] For more on the one-text procedure, see Roger Fisher, William Ury, and Bruce Patton, *Getting to Yes: Negotiating Agreement without Giving In* (New York: Penguin Books, 2011 revised edition).

[253] This account of Middletown and all the quotes are from Courtney E. Martin, "Stopping culture wars in their tracks: How one city did it," *Christion Science Monitor,* June 6, 2023, https://rb.gy/9ym58. It is very much worth reading in its entirety.

Then reality set in. At a board meeting early in Styles' tenure, a notoriously divisive figure in town took to the mic. "This woke CRT ideology is not education," he complained. "It's indoctrination. You'll give whatever fancy, flowery names you can to cover it up. But we all know it's CRT. You've awoken grassroots parents, mobilizing a movement to bring back common sense and stop division in this country."

Mr. Styles made no attempt to defend himself or the board. He just listened and took notes. At the end, he made a note to himself: *You gotta pick a fight against this if you want the kids to stay the main thing.* So when a video clip circulated of him saying "culturally responsive" and "equity," Mr. Styles posted his own video clarifying what he meant. When that only let loose a stream of nasty comments, he invited the most outraged to his office to talk through the facts. When that, too, did nothing to quell their rage, he knew he needed help.

> **And where better to find help in the midst of a culture war than among faith leaders whose native tongue is the language of values?**

After showing a video of the last board meeting to religious leaders at the Middletown Area Ministerial Alliance, Styles asked if it was representative of the community. "The ministers' response was an immediate and collective no. Their prescription? Remind the community of its capacity to keep the main thing as their main thing: the kids. Remind them, no matter the disagreements over theology or pedagogy or even public health, *all* belong."

The next school board meeting began like the last one, with the first person at the mic reading remarks, ideological in nature and legal in tone, repeating the complaints about CRT. Then something new happened. Reverend Michael Bailey came to the mic to remind the community of the values that bind them: strength, faith, love, respect, diversity, resilience, support, working together, the best interests of the children. Addressing the community, not the board or the superintendent, he said:

> Middletown is a strong city. It is strong because of our faith to love and respect one another. It is strong because of our diversity. Last but not least, it is strong because our students are resilient. . . . As a watchman on all of this strong city . . . my co-laborers of faith in Middletown are committed to extend our hands and our feet to support this institution to work together to do what's in the best interest of our children.

Then a second man came to the mic. "I would encourage the community to support elected leaders as much as possible," he said, "not without some criticism, legitimate criticism, but understanding these are complex issues and there needs to be nuance." The flood gates opened, and those typically on the periphery flooded in:

> A white woman with a pixie haircut spoke about being immunocompromised and urged people to think of the most vulnerable. A white doctor spoke of his great honor to treat the football team in his mask. A white local businessman, a member of the "positive gossipers," talked about how excited he was to hire well-prepared Middies and what a great job he thought the district was doing with Middletown's young people.
>
> It was as if, one public comment at a time, the frame on Middletown grew wider and wider and wider, the symbols more varied and beautiful. The disagreement over masks and history was still in the shot, but so were "watchman" Michael Bailey . . .
>
> The Middletown Area Ministerial Alliance, as well as "positive gossipers," showed up en force to eight school board meetings in a row and kept widening the frame.

In the end, it was those on the periphery of Middletown's culture wars that helped the community through them. They brought their faith and their friends to that task. Most of all, they brought a new perspective to the culture wars disrupting their kids' education. That peripheral vision is what widened the lens beyond masks and CRT and allowed them to see what those caught up in the battle and dominating the discourse could not see: the values and interests they all shared.

By the end, after each citizen had taken a turn at the mic, one after the other, week after week, they together conveyed one single message: they would be silenced no longer.

TWENTY-TWO

WORKING
from the
INSIDE
OUT

The history of humankind is a history of conflict, not just over land or material goods but over values. Sometimes those values are simply window dressing, used to justify material ends. But much of the time, values are, well, genuinely valued in their own right. They give us meaning; they influence the way we see ourselves and the world around us; they shape the course and contours of our lives; they define who we want to be and who we want to be with. Sometimes our values conflict with one another, causing so much internal turmoil that we push it aside and focus on the value conflicts boiling over around us. This essay explores how, by tending to the value conflicts within, we can better handle the value conflicts around us.

When deeply held values collide

Between 1993 and 2015, anti-abortion violence killed or wounded more than a dozen people within the United States. Three of those lives were ended on a December morning in 1994, when a gunman dressed in a black jacket and black pants stormed two abortion clinics in Brookline, Massachusetts.[254] At each

---

[254] Background presented here is based on Podziba Policy Mediation and the Essential Partners' website as well as Christopher B. Daley, "Gunman Kills 2, Wounds 5 in Attack on Abortion Clinics," *Washington Post*, December 31, 1994 and the activists' own account of the dialogues in "Talking with the Enemy," by Anne Fowler, Nicki Nichols Gamble, Frances X. Hogan, Melissa Kogut, Madeline McComish, and Barbara Thorp, *Boston Globe*, January 29, 2001. Please note: the Public Conversations Project is now Essential Partners, which has evolved and expanded upon the original approach.

clinic, he pulled out a semiautomatic .22-caliber rifle, shooting the reception-
ists at point-blank range, killing both of them and seriously wounding three
other people. The clinics had been targets of regular protests, some of which used
militant tactics, shouting at patients, handcuffing themselves to vehicles, and
blocking access to the clinics. It was the third fatal shooting at a U.S. abortion
clinic in just under two years.

For those on both sides of the abortion divide, the Brookline killings were
a painful wake-up call. Many activists on both sides knew something had to be
done to stave off violence. Family therapist Laura Chasin decided to be the someone who did something. It made sense for her to step up. Four years earlier, she
had cofounded the Public Conversations Project to see if techniques from family
therapy might improve public discourse on controversial topics like abortion.
Within eighteen months, the Project had tested this new approach in a series of
dialogues between pro-life and pro-choice activists and advocates.

After the Brookline killings, Chasin reached out to public policy mediator
Susan Podziba to partner with her on highly confidential dialogues between three
pro-choice and three pro-life activists. The meetings lasted for five-and-a-half
years. At the end, one pro-choice activist said the dialogues had "changed her
life," while a pro-life activist called the dialogues "a miracle."

While no one participating in the dialogues changed their fundamental beliefs
about abortion, their views grew far more complicated. Here's how Dr. Peter Coleman tells it in *The Way Out*:

> The profound respect, care, and love that grew between the women during their
> time together radically changed how they saw the members of the other camp
> . . . The personal stories shared and heard on both sides also expanded and com-
> plicated the leaders' understandings of the many issues involved with abortions
> (moral, legal, psychological, health-related, family, spiritual, and so on) and of
> the sometimes unintended consequences of their own activism.

In much the same way the congregants at BJ came to see Israel in a more
nuanced light, so did these activists come to see the choice to seek an abortion.[255]
And just as a pro-life participant in Sharon McMahon's Instagram workshop
came to question whether her beliefs should trump another person's autonomy, so did these activists come to see the inner contradictions in their beliefs

---

[255] For the story about BJ, see Essay 18: "Mending Our Frayed Social Fabric." For the full story, see
Ripley, *High Conflict*.

and the unintended consequences of their actions.[256] As a result, says Coleman, "their experiences of the issues, the others, and their own side became much more nuanced, much less one-sided, and therefore less closed, defensive, and destructive."[257]

Most of us are unaware of the value conflicts raging inside of us. If we are aware of anything, it is the inchoate sense of ill ease that accompanies the mixed feelings we have when confronting a moral dilemma that makes us feel "damned if we do and damned if we don't." Unresolved, those mixed feelings and the inner conflicts that fuel them grow intolerable. To relieve the pressure, we externalize the conflict by taking one side and outsourcing the other to people out there with whom we can battle more comfortably than we can with ourselves.

Since this leaves our internal conflicts unresolved, we have to keep turning them into external conflicts—the more entrenched the better—to distract us from our own ambivalence or guilt. Yet because these external conflicts can never resolve the conflicts within, they rage on, becoming forever wars.

We will always disagree over value-laden issues—and we should. They are complicated, and they matter. Still, acknowledging our inner conflicts and recognizing them in others gives us a better chance of breaking out of win-lose patterns and making common cause.

When conscious and unconscious values conflict

In the wake of earlier culture wars during the civil rights and anti-war movements, organizational scholars Chris Argyris and Donald Schön made a discomforting discovery. After interviewing a group of highly respected leaders about their values and theories of leadership, Argyris and Schön observed every single one of them act contrary to those values and theories when handling contentious issues. This was not just a matter of "not walking their talk." The data from their observations suggested that embedded in the leaders' actions, outside their awareness, was an unconscious "theory-in-use" informed by an equally unconscious set of "governing values" that included winning, staying in control, and saving face when challenged or threatened.[258] Shakespeare had it right: "I can easier teach

---

[256] See Essay 11: "Unlocking Our Minds" for the story about Sharon McMahon's Instagram workshop.

[257] Coleman, 215–216.

[258] Chris Argyris and Donald Schön, *Theory in Practice: Increasing Professional Effectiveness* (San Francisco: John Wiley & Sons, 1992). I studied and worked with Chris and Don for many years and co-authored *Action Science* with Chris Argyris and Robert Putnam in 1985.

twenty what were good to be done, than be one of the twenty to follow mine own teaching."[259]

Over the next decade, Chris and Don observed this same discrepancy between conscious and unconscious values in almost everyone they studied or taught, regardless of their gender, race, economic bracket, job, or any other demographic. They were stumped. They knew these governing values were not part of any formal curriculum taught in school, at home, or in church, nor was anyone aware of them. Eventually they surmised, as others have since, that these values were learned by example through an experiential, cultural curriculum hidden in everyday life. In this curriculum, all of us see the same patterned behavior every day as those around us act in a variety of ways to win, stay in control, and save face when challenged or threatened. Over time, we learn to follow suit, repeating the actions we have observed again and again until those actions and the values governing them move deep into "the rudimentary machinery of our minds," where they turn into automatic, unconscious habits.[260]

Most scientists used to think that such habits are so automatic that they lay outside our control, making them anywhere from hard to impossible to change. But recent research shows that our brains do not in fact relinquish all control. According to brain scientists at MIT, a small region in the brain's prefrontal cortex consciously controls which habits are switched on and when. "The value of a habit is you don't have to think about it. It frees up your brain to do other things," says MIT Professor Ann Graybiel. "However, it doesn't free up all of it. There's some piece of your cortex that's still devoted to that control."[261]

Those building on Chris and Don's original insight, myself included, discovered it is possible to exploit that little bit of control to become aware of our culturally learned social habits and develop new ones. We cannot do it alone, however. We need one another's help to "pierce the fog of our daily habits," as Rob Smith puts it in *Primal Fear*.[262] We need one another's help to see when our unconscious win-lose values are coaxing us into unwinnable wars over conscious

---

[259] William Shakespeare, *The Merchant of Venice.*

[260] Anne Trafton, "How the brain controls our habits: MIT neuroscientists identify a brain region that can switch between new and old habits," MIT News, October 29, 2012; Jerome Groopman, "Can Brain Science Help Us Break Bad Habits?" *New Yorker,* October 21, 2019. Also see Wendy Wood, *Good Habits, Bad Habits* (New York: Farrar, Straus and Giroux, 2019).

[261] Trafton, "How the brain controls our habits."

[262] Smith, *Primal Fear.*

values none of us consistently practices anyway. By helping one another, we can interrupt these dynamics and work together to create better ones.

Decades of research, my own and others, shows that by observing each other's actions, we can help one another see and change them, so we can make something good out of conflict.[263] Yogi Berra had it right: "You can observe a lot by just watching."

---

[263] Much has been written on how to shift these culturally learned social habits. See Appendix: Resources. Also go to the Constructive Dialogue Institute website for courses designed to cultivate new habits.

TWENTY-THREE

CANCELING LESS

to

LEARN MORE

Boston Review's editor-in-chief, Deborah Chasman, wanted to do the right thing, but what, exactly, was the right thing?[264] A day earlier, on May 4, 2018, writer Zinzi Clemmons had gone on Twitter to accuse Chasman's fiction editor, Pulitzer prize-winning author Junot Díaz, of cornering and forcibly kissing her at a workshop six years earlier.

On the heels of Clemmons' tweet, five other women took to social media to accuse Díaz of everything from "virulent misogyny" to "verbal sexual assault" to cheating on girlfriends to harshly criticizing their writing to asking his girlfriend to clean his kitchen to insulting a woman during a lunch meeting, then pulling her onto his lap when she started to cry. Within days, major outlets—the *Washington Post, Vox,* NPR, CNN—picked up and spread the story, amplifying but not investigating it.

All hell broke loose on social media, as calls for canceling Díaz spiraled: bookstores should ban his books; the Pulitzer committee should rescind his Pulitzer Prize and kick him off the committee; teachers should drop his books from their reading lists; conferences should disinvite him; he should be fired from the Massachusetts Institute of Technology (MIT), where he taught writing as a professor. Then Clemmons' husband tweeted: "Anyone looking for a fiction

---

[264] This account is based on Deborah Chasman, "My #MeToo Moment," *Chronicle of Higher Education,* April 17, 2023.

editor post? @Boston Review should be hiring fairly soon, at least as soon as @DebChasman & @jcohen570 catch up with the news. . . . Same goes for @MIT."

Chasman took the accusations seriously. "We knew #MeToo was changing the way we thought about abuses of power, and we wanted to do the right thing," she recalls. She also took fairness seriously and wanted to independently judge the facts of what happened. "We would have to make a decision about our magazine's association with Díaz, and we would have to do it under quickly intensifying public pressure."

In the end, after conducting an investigation that failed to corroborate the allegations, she and her co-editor, Joshua Cohen, announced their decision not to remove Díaz from his position as fiction editor at the *Boston Review*. "By the evening, social-media outrage started pouring in," Chasman recounts. "With hundreds of retweets and comments on our statement, only a tiny handful were supportive." One writer reached out to ask Chasman if she regretted her decision. "No, I replied. It was terrifying: We didn't know what the consequences would be, but changing our minds under pressure also seemed wrong."

Using value conflict to learn

Moral quandaries like the one Chasman faced over whether 'to cancel or not to cancel' Junot Díaz play out every day in far more private venues. Almost all of us have canceled or written off someone or some group at one time or another, so angry or distraught we cannot extend to them the fairness or kindness we believe they failed to extend to us. The cost is incalculable: relationships destroyed, people harmed, and few, if anyone, better off or wiser.

Canceling across groups is much easier to pull off than canceling within groups. Those in other groups are so distant from us that we cannot easily understand why they did what they did or empathize. Canceling people within groups is up close and personal and much harder. Most of us will only do it if we think someone has betrayed or abandoned our group's values or beliefs.

Chasman got caught in the crosshairs of both in-group and cross-group canceling. As a feminist, she could easily be seen by her fellow feminists as abandoning the value of solidarity with the #MeToo movement. As a White woman in a position of power, she could easily be seen as a member of a more privileged group who could not appreciate what the women of color accusing Díaz were up against. She was the perfect target for getting canceled, and she knew it.

Five years after the fact, in April 2023, Chasman published an account of her experience in the *Chronicle of Higher Education,* after both the *New York Times Magazine* and the *New Republic* first scheduled, then dropped the essay. In "My #MeToo Moment," Chasman describes in detail how she tried to "navigate the conflict between wanting to support the #MeToo movement and resisting what it seemed to call for." Looking back, she knew she had made mistakes and still had much to learn. For that reason alone, her account of what she felt, thought, and did is a master class in how to sustain learning while navigating internal and external value conflicts with integrity. The steps she took, summarized below, have much to teach us about how to navigate and learn from the moral dilemmas we face in public and private life.[265]

1. Refuse to simplify; face complexity head on. As soon as Chasman learned of Clemmons' accusation, she knew she would have to make a decision about Díaz's future. It was a grueling moment. Her different roles and identities—as an editor, a feminist, a colleague, and an employer—were all pulling her in different directions, as were her values and principles, all of it obscuring the way forward. "It raised hard questions: about the role of journalists and social media in movements for justice; about the nature of public decision-making when there are no established guidelines for judgment, and when what is at stake stretches well beyond civil and criminal legal standards to a vision of social transformation; and even about what stories are for—how narratives of harm can create social change."

She struggled to find her bearings. The pull to give in to anxiety, to simplify the situation, and to act before thinking must have been overwhelming. To resist that pull, she had to rely on the courage of her convictions: "We edit a magazine of public reason, committed for the last 30 years to the idea that democracy depends on public discussion and that people of good will can disagree. Either giving in to pressure or ignoring the allegations—doing nothing and letting it blow over, as some had advised us to—would have been profoundly at odds with our mission." She would follow her convictions into the breach rather than cave to pressure.

2. Explore what happened, casting a wide net. Chasman and Cohen most wanted to know if something had happened on their watch at the *Boston Review.* So far, no one had investigated any of the allegations, so they would have to start from scratch and launch their own inquiry. Looking to sexual-harassment law,

[265] Chasman, "My #MeToo Moment."

they decided to cast a wide net, looking for a pattern of behavior. They started with the women writers who had had the most contact with Díaz. After inviting them to share their experiences in confidence, by phone or correspondence, almost a dozen women got back to say Díaz had done nothing inappropriate with them, nor had they heard of any wrongdoing. "Some said they were afraid to speak out publicly against what they saw as viral character assassination. A few expressed relief that I had reached out. In an email, the writer Shivani Manghnani, whom Díaz edited for *Boston Review*, wrote, 'I can't say enough about how his work and teaching changed my life. *Saved my life.*'"

When Chasman then called people who had worked with Díaz, she heard nothing comparable to Clemmons' accusation of forcible kissing. She did hear that he took over conversations at dinner parties and that he kissed cheeks, as is the custom in the Dominican Republic where he was raised. At the two places Díaz taught—MIT and Voices of Our Nations Arts (VONA)—where the public accusations prompted investigations, Chasman uncovered no allegations of sexual misconduct, only an alumni letter at VONA accusing the administration of allowing widespread sexual, emotional, and verbal abuse and assaults "by Díaz and other faculty" with no instances cited.

She also listened to a tape recording of Carman Maria Machado's 2012 interaction with Díaz during a Q&A at a University of Iowa event, which Machado referred to in a tweet as a "blast of misogynist rage and public humiliation." On the tape, Chasman heard Machado ask Díaz how he could write a character with "borderline sociopathic disregard for everyone he fucks." His answer, which Chasman thought could come across as patronizing, did not strike her at all as a "blast of misogynist rage and public humiliation."

3. *Make sense of conflicting accounts; get help on the dilemmas they raise.*
Far from alleviating Chasman's worries, the results of the investigation only deepened them. "Everything seemed to be run together, blurring the distinctions we usually draw between hurtful behavior and sexual violence, between jerks and abusers, between authors and their work. . . . I struggled with the suggestion that he was a misogynist hiding in plain sight, that his work [mentoring women writers] was a mask cynically adopted to prey on women."

With no evidence that Díaz had abused his position at *Boston Review*, Chasman and Cohen were now leaning toward retaining Díaz, but worried about harming the #MeToo movement or victims of sexual violence. To get help, Chasman called two friends, a historian of radical social movements and a therapist who worked with victims of violence. After talking through her worries, both women reassured her that "social movements should and could withstand critique."

4. Explore options with others in light of different values and pressures. Chasman and Cohen saw three options: say nothing, fire Díaz, or wait for a more thorough investigation. None of them satisfied what they took to be their "ethical obligation" to explain their reasoning. They thought it was a complicated situation that called for a nuanced, complicated explanation. They wanted to report with precision and transparency that their due diligence did not uncover a compelling reason to fire Díaz. They wanted to explain that the issues their investigation did uncover around power imbalances were grounds for discussion, not termination.

They drafted two dozen versions of a possible statement. Before finalizing the draft, they tested it with others at the journal, many of whom were concerned. Among them were the poetry editors who advised them to put Díaz on leave and see how things played out. They thought it unwise to "adjudicate" the movement by drawing a line between what was and was not an offense bad enough to warrant firing. Another employee agreed that Díaz ought not be fired for Twitter allegations, but said she didn't want to "die on that hill." Neither did Chasman or Cohen, but they had no choice. They had to make a decision, and in making a decision, they would have to draw a line between behavior that did and did not warrant firing. "If we are adjudicating," Cohen said, "then everyone is adjudicating."

5. Make a decision, explain your reasoning, and acknowledge other views. In light of what Chasman and Cohen heard at the journal, they revised the draft, clarifying that not everyone associated with the *Boston Review* agreed with all they said in the letter. On June 5, 2018, they posted the statement, acknowledging the issues were complex and that reasonable people committed to gender equality and fighting bias in the publishing industry might come to different conclusions. "Our obligation," they explained, "is to give this serious issue thoughtful consideration, listen carefully, consider the substance of the allegations, weigh the different things we have heard, acknowledge our own predispositions and potential biases, and make our best judgment. We take this obligation seriously and hope we have discharged it properly."

6. Wait for it. Chasman and Cohen's statement was instantly met by public rebuke, and the poetry editors resigned, issuing a public statement critical of the decision. The impact on Chasman was brutal: "As countless people have testified, mass online shaming is emotionally, mentally, and physically devastating. Unable to sleep for days, I feared I'd missed something—that I had harmed survivors, that I had damaged our magazine, that I had compromised my own feminist convictions, that I had stood in the movement's way, hurting all of us."

Then, slowly, over months, new information emerged in several different outlets, showing that those who had attacked Díaz on social media had—*wait for it*—unfairly rushed to judgment.

On June 14, in a *New York Magazine* essay by Lila Shapiro on Carman Maria Machado's work, Shapiro questioned Machado's account of Díaz's "enraged" twenty-minute rant during the 2012 event at the University of Iowa. Shapiro had played the recording of the session for several of her colleagues, all of whom thought Díaz sounded "perfectly polite; didactic, but appropriately so, for a lecture." On June 30, 2018, the *Boston Globe* published an investigative report by Mark Shanahan and Stephanie Ebbert that reported how many of the allegations against Díaz had "withered under scrutiny" and that the predicted deluge of stories about Díaz had never materialized. On November 28, 2022, *Semafor* founder Ben Smith interviewed four 2018 Pulitzer board members about the allegations against Díaz, and according to them, their lawyers had confirmed that Díaz's "forcible" kiss was on Clemmons' cheek.

7. Reflect on your mistakes; retain the right to learn. Despite these revelations, Chasman still wondered whether she had, in the end, done the right thing in the right way. She knew she had made a few missteps along the way. In hindsight, she thought it would have been better to put Díaz on leave while investigating the allegations, and she regretted not talking directly with Clemmons. In the hope of learning more, she reached out to several women who thought she had made the wrong decision. Some of the conversations went well; one did not. She faulted herself for getting defensive in that conversation, for asking the wrong questions and failing to ask an important one. She used this self-scrutiny, not to beat herself up but to retain the right to learn. That stance allowed her to come to terms with the past while framing up a future challenge: "How do we act on stories of harm in our personal and professional lives without inviting more punitive regimes? How do we work simultaneously to advance accountability and justice?"

What does all this mean for us?

Even now, after her own public shaming, Chasman hopes that "critique and conversation can move us toward justice, collectively." Our current cancel culture makes it terribly hard to sustain that hope, to keep learning, and to move toward justice. With help from others and the courage of her convictions, however, Chasman managed to do it. In the end, she modeled for all of us how to see the victim in the perpetrator and the perpetrator in the victim, and how to ensure that accountability does not deprive others of the justice and freedom we claim for ourselves.

Still, she wishes she had read the work of author and activist adrienne maree brown while making her way through cancel-culture hell. In *We Will Not Cancel Us,* brown imagines a form of accountability and justice that is more transformative than punitive, that gets at the root of harm and heals both those suffering from and perpetrating harm. It is an ambitious vision. But perhaps only an ambitious vision can move us past our ingrained tendency to fight *against* each other rather than fighting *for* something we all need and want: a person, a community, a nation we can trust because they behave fairly. If there is a moral to this story, then, perhaps it is this:

> **We have met the enemy, and it is us. "If you want to make peace with your enemy," said Nelson Mandela, "you have to work with your enemy. Then he becomes your partner."**

To create a more just world, we will need to make peace with ourselves. We will need to partner with the enemy within. All of us fall short of the values we hold dear. None of us walks our talk. All of us have grown up in a mainstream culture that predisposes us to commit sins of omission and commission, even when (or especially when) holding others accountable for *their* sins. If we can accept that painful but ultimately liberating truth, we will have reason to hope.

TWENTY-FOUR

USING THE PAST
to BUILD
a BETTER FUTURE

In *Learning from the Germans,* philosopher Susan Neiman raises a question that has sparked some of our most divisive culture battles: "What is our responsibility to our national pasts?" That question prompted Neiman, raised in Atlanta, Georgia, and now living in Germany, to record hundreds of hours of interviews with Germans who played major roles in "contesting and reframing" a past marked by the extermination of six million Jews and an untold number of "undesirables." Neiman wanted to see what, if anything, people in the United States might learn from Germans about how to come to terms with their own past, one marked by the enslavement of ten million African Americans and the displacement and extermination of millions of Indigenous Peoples. In the end, she came to believe that the reason a majority of Germans are now able to resist factions and forces intent on repeating history is because, although horrendously painful, they confronted and learned from their past.[266] An earlier article of Neiman's that reached the same conclusion prompted an American to write her a letter:

> I have lived in Mississippi my entire life (Oxford now) and I am a white conservative. . . . I—and many like me—genuinely do wonder what the right thing to do is with regard to the history of the southern states in America and the history of the United States in general. . . .
>
> What do you think? Should we tear down all Confederate statues? Should we rename all buildings and streets? Should we take this cleansing past things relating to the Civil War and take Washington off the dollar bill? For your

---

[266] Susan Neiman, *Learning from the Germans: Race and the Memory of Evil* (New York: Farrar, Straus and Giroux, 2019), Kindle Ed., 148.

reference, I have asked numerous alleged civil rights leaders in Mississippi, and I even had the opportunity to eat dinner with James Meredith and hear his take on the issue. The sides are split, but man oh man, those who think we need to eliminate all vestiges of the slavery era are the angriest. But are they right?

The question of whether "they" or anyone else is "right" is the kind of question that turns culture wars into forever wars. No mutually acceptable answer to that question can ever be found as long as some of us see only our flag, others only its shadow, each side making contradictory claims, both of which seem plausible to some, neither of which can be proved for all.

Using the past to think about the future

A different question posed by Neiman holds more promise. To paraphrase: "How should, and should not, our past be used in thinking about our moral and political futures?"[267] It is a great question, yet it cannot be answered if all we do is fight over how to interpret and teach the past, which many news stories suggest we do. Commentator David French went beyond those stories to discover research showing "a remarkable amount of consensus on what should be taught—whether the topic is the sins of America's past or the virtues of our founding documents."[268] In fact, one More in Common study found that, far from wanting to ban accounts of our nation's failings, most of us have "little appetite for shielding students from US history's uglier chapters. Most agree that books with content that may offend people should not be removed from schools or libraries, but rather left for students to grapple with."[269] This suggests that while a vocal minority is agitating to ban books and curricula that critically examine our past, many more of us consider such examination an act of patriotism (see Table 24.1).[270]

These findings make me wonder: Why are we not hearing more from these voices, and what can we do to help those within this quieter majority speak more freely? How can we help those around us not look away from our past but use it to create a better future?

James Baldwin devoted his life to confronting our past, so we could construct a more just future. In one way or another, he cautioned us again and again: "People

---

[267] Ibid., 19.

[268] French, "Activism and Apathy."

[269] Ibid.

[270] From More in Common's Juneteenth American Identity Research Project, May–June 2022.

Table 24.1: Critically Examining Our History

The majority of Americans across race and political ideology also believe that critically examining our history is an act of patriotism.

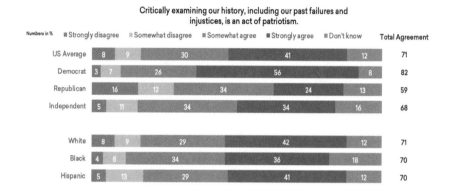

Question: To what extent do you agree or disagree with the following statements?
Source: More in Common

There is strong support across generations that critically examining our history is an act of patriotism.

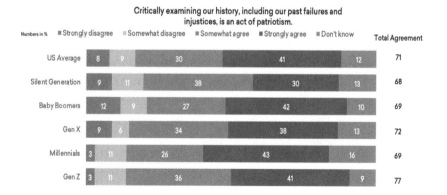

Question: To what extent do you agree or disagree with the following statements?
Source: More in Common

Source: More in Common's Juneteenth American Identity Research Project who imagine that history flatters them are impaled on their history like a butterfly on a pin and become incapable of seeing or changing themselves, or the world."

What does it mean to examine our past?

We have always lived so far apart from one another, each in our own groups, that it is easy to use the past to flatter or to fool ourselves. So any truthful encounter with the past must begin with the facts, but it cannot end there. We must also reflect on ourselves and on what we make of the facts—and why. So the question is not only "what do these facts tell me about our past?" but "why am I focusing on these facts and not on others, and what do my interpretations of the facts say about me, my values, and my beliefs?" Eddie Glaude illustrates the point in *Begin Again*:

> For some, the fact that Washington and Jefferson owned slaves disqualifies them as moral exemplars. For others, the men may have been wrong in owning slaves, but that fact stands alongside other, more admirable aspects of their lives. . . . Each of these interpretations reveals something about what is valued, and about how the past as told speaks to the present. Our appeals to history can never be entirely objective; they aim, just as often, to clarify our commitments today."[271]

Today's repetitious arguments over how to interpret and teach our past and over what facts to select and ignore are at the heart of our culture wars. Among those wars' many casualties is one set of facts from our history that we almost never acknowledge or teach, namely this:

> **Ever since our nation's founding, those with more political and economic power have sought to divide those with less power to keep or increase their power, while those with less power have repeatedly succumbed to these ploys in a desperate effort not to lose power. The result is a widening gap between those with more or less political and economic power.**

That is why words written by W.E.B. DuBois almost a hundred years ago remain true today:

> There probably are not today in the world two groups of workers with practically identical interests who hate and fear each other so deeply and persistently and who are kept so far apart that neither sees anything of common interest.

---

[271] Eddie S. Glaude, Jr., *Begin Again: James Baldwin's America and Its Urgent Lessons for Our Own* (New York: Crown, 2020).

The result of this [division] was that the wages of both classes could be kept low, the Whites fearing to be supplanted by Negro labor, the Negroes always being threatened by the substitution of White labor.[272]

In the time before and since DuBois penned those words, we have spent more time fighting *against* one another to *stop something* than we have spent time fighting *with* one another to *create something* that works better for all of us.

If we continue to use the past to litigate who was good or bad, or who had it better or worse, we will continue to be impaled on our history like Baldwin's pinned butterfly.

Susan Neiman spent months exploring the way two nations confronted pasts that sought to exploit or extinguish differences. In the end, she concluded, "Above all, we must acknowledge our shared vulnerability to the silliest banalities of evil. . . . That acknowledgment makes it possible to critically examine our own histories without tribalism or trauma."[273]

Our society will always be taxed by racism and its cousins, from sexism to homophobia to class prejudice and so on. It is a costly tax, one that chips away every day at our souls as a people and our moral foundation as a nation. Still, we are unlikely to ever eliminate it entirely. "The urge to blame your troubles on strangers is too old and too deep," says Neiman. "That means we shall always have to weed it out wherever it sprouts. It is an invasive species that will choke off all those other plants that bring us joy and sustenance."[274]

That continual weeding will always be our individual and collective responsibility as a people. As Václav Havel put it, "Position in the power hierarchy . . . gives no one unlimited responsibility and guilt, nor does it completely absolve anyone."[275]

---

[272] W.E.B. DuBois, *Black Reconstruction in American 1860–1880* (New York: Free Press, 1998), 700, cited in Heather McGhee, *The Sum of Us,* 126. My emphasis.

[273] Neiman, 384.

[274] Neiman, 358.

[275] Havel, *The Power of the Powerless.*

IT TAKES PASSION, NOT NUMBERS

The oft-cited Stockdale Paradox about persevering in the face of adversity comes from Vice Admiral James Stockdale's experience as a prisoner of war in Việt Nam in the Hỏa Lò Prison, dubbed the Hanoi Hilton by Americans. The prison was first built by the French to hold Vietnamese fighting for independence in the first half of the twentieth century. Many of those leading the communist movement in Việt Nam spent time there in the 1930s and 1940s. By the 1960s, some of those imprisoned by the French were leading the regime imprisoning the Americans who had followed in France's wake. Stockdale was one of those Americans. He spent close to three thousand days and nights in that prison camp between 1965 and 1973, where he lived in subhuman conditions and suffered torture routinely. Not everyone who spent time there survived with their minds or bodies intact, if they survived at all. James Stockdale did.

When business author Jim Collins asked how he survived, Stockdale responded: "I never lost faith in the end of the story. I never doubted not only that I would get out, but also that I would prevail in the end and turn the experience into the defining event of my life, which, in retrospect, I would not trade." That faith, he said, was very different from that of the "optimists," as Stockdale called them.

The optimists would say, "We're going to be out by Christmas." Then Christmas would come, and Christmas would go, then Easter, then Thanksgiving, then Christmas again. Each time, they set their sights on a date and the date would pass.

They died, Stockdale said, of a broken heart. "You must never confuse faith that you will prevail in the end—which you can never afford to lose—with the discipline to confront the most brutal facts of your current reality, whatever they might be."[276]

---

[276] Jim Collins, *Good to Great: Why Some Companies Make the Leap . . . and Others Don't* (New York: Harper Business, 2011), quoted by Boris Groysberg and Robin Abrahams in "What the Stockdale Paradox Tells Us About Crisis Leadership," *Harvard Business Review,* August 17, 2020.

That is the Stockdale Paradox. These are our brutal facts:

- We face two existential threats: tyranny and extinction.

- Both threats call upon us to radically restructure the space between us, so we can cooperate across groups on overcoming them.

- Powerful forces inside and outside of us will thwart us at every turn, seeking to divide us to dilute our power and to preserve the status quo.

Overcoming the brutal facts

Social movements throughout history have served as the vehicle through which those with less power have overcome brutal facts and changed the world. Today a new movement is afoot to build a multigroup democracy that can usher in a better future for all of us, not just some of us. Realizing this pluralist vision of democracy is—and will always be—a chaotic, complicated, and constantly shifting challenge. No singular approach or group can meet it. It requires a multifaceted movement that is greater than the sum of its parts.

Few understand this better than Julia Roig of the Horizons Project. After spending three decades in Latin America and the Balkans on peacebuilding efforts, she found the biggest need was not securing more money for one or another group but creating more coordination among them.[277] That's why she founded the Horizon Project, where she connects bridge-builders and peace-builders, groups advancing social justice and those working to protect democratic processes and norms. She hopes to forge out of these different approaches a common path forward to overcome the many forces dividing us.

Creating that common path forward will not be easy. Tensions abound, especially between those seeking unity and peace and those seeking justice, igniting internecine wars like those within the #MeToo movement or at New College. Yet as Rachel Kleinfeld and Shamil Idriss point out, these conflicts ignore "the power of collaborative action to transform conflict, restore democracy, and promote peace. Such collaborative approaches yield a dual benefit: meaningful progress toward social justice and improved trust between otherwise opposing groups. Activists who facilitate collaborative action do not treat

---

[277] "Julia Roig and the Horizons Project on Weaving a Health Democracy," *Beyond Intractability* Newsletter #87, February 23, 2023, https://rb.gy/ex7zu.

justice and peace as a tradeoff but integrate the principles of both in their activism."[278]

Social movements have always suffered from the same divisive forces dividing our democracy. Those forces will constantly conspire against us to maintain systems that serve too few of us and threaten the survival of all of us. We must be equally constant in return. We must take the best from each of us and discard the worst in all of us. We must face the brutal facts while sustaining faith and hope, especially in one another, independent of a timeline we cannot predict. Most of all, we must never forget what Baldwin said: "You don't need numbers, you need passion." With the commitment, determination, and perseverance that passion sustains, we can achieve a common vision, no matter the obstacles. History tells us so, time and again.

The history of those "who were few"

It was Christmas night in 1776 when General George Washington and his troops reached the Delaware River. People across the colonies were losing hope for independence as their confidence in the Continental Army waned. Washington himself was aware of the brutal facts.[279] For months, his army had been in steady retreat, losing one battle after another. Washington's troops were dwindling by the day. In December, he was down to roughly 5,000 men, only 3,000 of them fit for duty. On the other side of the Delaware were the British with 25,000 men, 30,000 if needed. As Washington peered across the river, a slight drizzle turned to freezing rain and then snow, driven by a piercing wind.

"Look, it's over," someone told Washington. "We've lost."

But Washington refused to see it that way, said historian David McCullough in an interview at Washington's home in Mount Vernon. "If there was a more courageous human being who ever lived, I don't know who it was. It was the courage of his convictions. He would not quit. *Every* sign was that it was over, you've lost, give up, it's not worth it. But no, he would not stop." Washington would not stop because his vision was clear and his passion unwavering: he was determined to beat the enemy and establish democracy in America.

---

[278] Shamil Idriss and Rachel Kleinfeld, "No One Is Right in the Debate for and Against Philanthropic Pluralism," *Chronicle of Philanthropy*, June 15, 2023.

[279] Based on a must-read interview with David McCullough at Washington's home at Mt. Vernon, https://rb.gy/im2ti.

"So he did what one often has to do when all hope is gone," McCullough recounts. "He attacked." After crossing the Delaware, he struck at Trenton, and won, then turned around and struck at Princeton, and won. That neither engagement was a significant battle was of no consequence. What mattered was that they had defeated their much larger, more formidable enemy. That one fact overshadowed all others and boosted morale throughout the country.

McCullough believes that this moment was *the* turning point, not just in the revolution or in our nation's history but in world history, because the world would never to be the same again.

In taking stock of Washington and his men "who were few," as McCullough put it, he saw some "force inside" that allowed them to create a turning point out of adversity. You can see that same force in Henry Knox as he and his men made their way from Fort Ticonderoga across snow-covered mountains and half-frozen rivers to Boston; in college students Matthew Stephenson, Moshe Ashe, Juan Elias, Allison Gornick, and Derek Black who, despite the outrage of their peers, built relationships powerful enough to transform entrenched beliefs; in trailblazers like Mary Parker Follett and Costa Rican diplomat Christiana Figueres who discovered ways to make something good out of the most intractable conflicts; in researchers like Larry Diamond and James Fishkin and those at More in Common who generate insights we can use to build a stronger nation and a better democracy; in the old and new, White and Black Mainers who showed us how to build powerful multiracial coalitions despite the many forces seeking to divide us; in James Baldwin's and Václav Havel's insistence on living within the truth even while living in a system of lies; in Sharon McMahon who converted frustration with misinformation into an Instagram site that uses verifiable facts to bring over a million citizens together to learn with one another; in those at Braver Angels who are calling on Americans to rise up and build a citizens movement with them; in those at One Step and Resetting the Table who are reducing the affective polarization that gives rise to hate and division; in the people of Billings, Montana, who spontaneously came together after attacks on their neighbors to say in unison: Not In Our Town; in the people of Pittsburgh who repaired their world by befriending each other in the wake of the worst antisemitic attack in U.S. history; in filmmakers like Patrice O'Neill and her filmmaking team who document how communities like Pittsburgh and Billings are standing up to hate and building the local checks and balances our democracy needs today; in the solutions journalists, restorative narratives, and digital innovators who are reinventing the practice and business of journalism, so it informs and engages rather than exhausts and enrages; in leaders like Deborah Chasman who draw on the courage of their convictions to put themselves in harm's way for the sake of justice; in members of Congress like Representatives Kilmer, Graves, Timmons, and their colleagues on the Modernization of Congress committee who make friends across parties so they can make progress for the American people; and in the thousands of citizens launching, leading, joining, and supporting organizations across our nation, bringing groups together to learn from each other and work together on building a better future for all of us.

Beyond the barricades

I find hope in all of these stories and in my own life, when I reach across divides and see in others—and allow them to see in me—the common humanity that will be our saving grace.

In the chaos and mayhem around us, I find hope in the possibility that we are witnessing the last dying gasps of a fading order and the birth of a new one, one that reflects the truth in Dr. Martin Luther King Jr.'s words, "We are all caught in an inescapable network of mutuality, tied into a single garment of destiny. Whatever affects one directly, affects all indirectly."

Perhaps most of all, I find hope in the next generation to whom we are passing a battered baton. Among them is an eighteen-year-old high school senior from rural Upstate New York who gave a Valedictory speech in 2022. Like many of her generation, she is pinning her hopes and her future on our working together to remake ourselves and the world around us. Let us rise with her:

> Having hope is never stupid. No matter how buried it gets or how lost you feel, you must hold on to hope, keep it alive. We have to be greater than what we suffer.
>
> To manifest our dreams, we must create: Create art, relationships, communities, safe spaces, discussions, policy changes. Continue to make things. To build anew is the truest form of strength and defiance one can possibly harness.
>
> As we move on to the next chapter of our lives, we enter into a world constructed on the basis of a series of systems that are far from perfect. . . . The days of inequity, discrimination, and hatred can end, but only if every one of us fights for the fair treatment of all humans.
>
> It is our fight. I know that we can win. I know that greatness lies in every one of us. From here on, history has its eyes on you.

Let us be the ones who set the past ablaze to bathe in the glow of the future . . . There is a world we long to see beyond the barricade of what we have always known. We can see the way the world could be in spite of the way it is.

It will only arrive if we rise up, if we decide we are past patiently waiting for much needed change and decide to take up action ourselves. Fight for what matters to you no matter what. Even if we fall short, even if we fail, what better way is there to live?

The world will be saved and remade by the dreamers. Let us together rebuild this world that we may share in the days of peace.[280]

---

[280] Written and delivered by Autumn Fleming at her 2021 high school graduation in Upstate New York. Autumn is currently attending Pace University, where she is majoring in communications and media studies.

ACKNOWLEDGMENTS

In a 1981 speech to the Ohio Arts Council, Toni Morrison said, "If there's a book that you want to read, but it hasn't been written yet, then you must write it." I am indebted to Morrison for these words. They sustained me for eighteen months of writing as "a way of thinking—not just feeling but thinking about things that are disparate, unresolved, mysterious, problematic, or just sweet," as Morrison put it. Many writers kept me company during this project. All of them inspired me to keep trying to say something that might be useful to others. It was a privilege and a pleasure to spend so much time with them. It was also empowering to discover how many of them were women and people of color who had, by necessity, forged new ways of seeing and doing things to free themselves, especially their minds, from the constraints that society had placed on them by virtue of their gender or race. I gratefully acknowledge their work and my own limitations in doing justice to it.

Friendship is a theme that runs throughout this book. It also made the book possible. I have been blessed throughout life with extraordinary friends, but none more extraordinary than those who showed up again and again over the eighteen months I worked on this project: Jamie Higgins, David Diamond, Yordanos Eyoel, Kim Syman, Jeff Wetzler, Susan Asiyanbi, Kevin Ozenne, Rachel Schankula, Josh Anderson, Jennifer Goldman-Wetzler, Richard Barth, Bill Noonan, Bob Putnam, Lori Russell, J.B. Lyon, and my godsons, Jack and Nick Daley. All read and commented on drafts, spotted mistakes and oversights, raised concerns and made suggestions, took on the occasional task, connected me with resources, and always rooted me on.

To all those friends who made a solitary task less lonely, I am deeply grateful. Amy Edmondson, George Daley, Fatimah Burnam-Watkins and her family, Phil McArthur and Amy Meltzer, Elisa Villanueva-Beard, Nell Kisiel, Lisa Byrne, Kathy and Leo DeNatale, Elizabeth Riker, Sarah and Jeffrey Adams, Carol Crane, Sally Booth and Jeffrey Cole, Morgan and Allie Kelly, Mary Scriber, Janet Crowder, Peter Cooper, Steve and Jenn Kimball (and, of course, Tanner) all kept my spirits up by asking after me and the book while sharing a meal, going for a walk, or trekking up to Vermont to pull me out of my solitary existence.

Scholars Jenny Mansbridge, Sameer Srivastava, Victor Friedman, and Samar Ali as well as solution journalist David Bornstein were remarkably generous with their time. I am grateful to each of them for keeping me and the manuscript grounded in reality with their helpful corrections and suggestions.

My advisory work with the Rebuild Congress Initiative (RCI) gave me unusual insight into what it takes to move an unwieldy, multi-ton boulder up a long, steep hill in treacherous weather. Over the past few years, I have watched in wonder as RCI defied the odds and made a difference in Congress that few, including me, thought possible. By tethering their hopes to a well-organized, collaborative effort, they did what we all need to do: forgo coercion and instant transformation in favor of working over time alongside a wide range of different people and groups to create meaningful, sustainable change together.

Among my most cherished friends, I count my brothers. Their efforts to strengthen our democracy and protect our planet reach back without interruption to our youth. After decades of raising money for political causes and candidates early in his career, my brother Rob most recently wrote the inspiring and insightful *Primal Fear: Tribalism, Empathy, and the Way Forward* (2021). And after decades of work in the leadership transformation business, my brother Tony is still dedicating himself to saving our planet, most recently through 2030 or Bust. My brother Michael, who served our nation in the army, gave me the financial help I needed to send this book off into the world. In May 2022, Mike died unexpectedly of a heart attack, making this book our joint legacy. I will always be grateful to our parents, Jane and McLain Smith, for instilling in all of us a sense of responsibility for the world around us and imbuing our lives with unshakeable meaning and purpose as a result.

Writing this book was similar to raising a child. I found its childhood delightful, its puberty challenging, and its adolescence a living hell. I was only too happy to send it off into the world by its end. I am certain I would not have made it through without the help of colleagues like Andrew Doty of RCI who did superb research and offered useful critiques along the way. Both were invaluable, as was his initial draft of the essay "Outwitting Misinformation." Nicole Levine at RCI connected me with the talented Maryn Hiscott, whose reading and research over the summer of 2022 allowed me to extend the scope of the project. Award-winning filmmaker and Not In Our Town founder, Patrice O'Neill, gave me early access to her exceptional documentary *Repairing the World*. As thankful as I am for that help, I am most thankful for her tenacious efforts over three decades to empower citizens across our nation to act more like "upstanders" than bystanders so we, the people, can be stronger than hate.

The team at Ballast Books did a brilliant job of shepherding me and this manuscript through the publishing process. The collaboration, competence, and care demonstrated by this up-start hybrid publishing company is in a league of its own. Acquisitions editor Kat Dixon and production manager Kayleigh Rucinski were unflagging in their enthusiasm for the project and delivered the goods whenever I needed a creative way to get something done. Copy editor Tara Taylor took great care with the manuscript, finding errors and fixing awkward phrases, all of which improved the manuscript.

As a constructive disruptor, Ballast is one of the best. They even managed to track down Vadym Malyshevskyi, the artist living in Ukraine who created the image for the book's cover, so I could inquire about a similar logo. I began my email to Vadym by saying what an inspiration Ukraine is for all of us in the United States who are also fighting for democracy. Less than an hour later, he wrote back:

> I, in turn, want to express my gratitude for the assistance provided by the United States and the American people. We really appreciate it. I live in Kyiv, and when there was a barbaric massive shelling of our city several times before my eyes, your "Patriot" air defense systems shot down all the missiles, which saved the lives of many people and possibly my family. Thank you.

I am grateful to Vadym Malyshevskyi not only for creating such a brilliant image but for reminding me and all of us what we are fighting for and why.

My dearest friend and husband, Bruce Patton, served throughout as my most trusted advisor, thought partner, editor, wife whisperer, connector, promoter, confidant, world-class chef, and pinch-hitting dog walker. His belief in this book was matched only by his belief in me and our marriage. Despite working long hours at RCI, he still managed to get the manuscript to a remarkable group of readers whose comments and support for the book mean the world to us.

While I wrote this book, I kept coming across a passage from the Talmud. Its wisdom comforted me whenever doubt set in. I now pass it on to you: "You are not obligated to complete the work, but neither are you free to desist from it (2:21)."

Diana McLain Smith
October 2023

I began my life's work in two communities on opposite sides of Boston, one predominantly Black, the other predominantly White, both made up of hard-working, low-income families. For twelve years, I worked alternately as a counselor, a journalist, and a community organizer alongside people struggling to navigate circumstances largely stacked against them. Where they went, I went—to their homes, their schools, the streets, the courts, and prison. It was a ten-year master class in hard-earned resilience on the one hand and learned helplessness on the other.

During this time, I received my bachelor's degree at Boston University in an independent, interdisciplinary program called Social Writing in America. Five years later, I went to graduate school at Harvard University, where I earned my doctoral degree at an interdisciplinary program that integrated theory, research, and practice. While there, I studied and intervened in systems as diverse as families, organizations, communities, and, in one instance, a nation as they each struggled to adapt to new demands and shifting circumstances. I also began life-long collaborations with founders in the fields of organizational learning, negotiation, and systems change, including Chris Argyris, Donald Schön, Roger Fisher, Bruce Patton, and David Kantor.

Over the past thirty-five years, I have led change efforts in some of America's most iconic businesses and entrepreneurial nonprofits. During that time, I built an approach to systems change called Leading through Relationships (LTR)™ that is now used in organizations around the world to convert debilitating intergroup conflict into a constructive force for change.

At the Monitor Group, a top-tier global strategy firm, I chaired Monitor University where I taught LTR and conducted research for two books. As chief executive partner of the venture philanthropy firm New Profit, I led a two-year culture change effort that enabled future growth.

I am the coauthor of *Action Science* with Chris Argyris and Robert Putnam (Jossey-Bass) and the author of *Divide or Conquer* (Penguin) and *The Elephant in the Room* (Wiley) as well as dozens of articles, including "Building Adaptive Relationships," "Changing a Culture's DNA," "Action Science Revisited," and "Too Hot to Handle" with Amy Edmondson.

I share my life with my husband of thirty years, Bruce Patton, coauthor of the bestsellers *Getting to YES* and *Difficult Conversations*.